The
Gladiators

The
Gladiators

History's Most Deadly Sport

Fik Meijer

Translated from the Dutch by
Liz Waters

THOMAS DUNNE BOOKS
ST. MARTIN'S PRESS ❧ NEW YORK

THOMAS DUNNE BOOKS.
An imprint of St. Martin's Press.

THE GLADIATORS. Copyright © 2003, 2004 by Fik Meijer. Map copyright
© Jan ter Haar 2003, 2004. All rights reserved. Printed in the United
States of America. No part of this book may be used or reproduced in any
manner whatsoever without written permission except in the case of brief
quotations embodied in critical articles or reviews. For information,
address St. Martin's Press, 175 Fifth Avenue, New York, N.Y. 10010.

www.stmartins.com

Library of Congress Cataloging-in-Publication Data

Meijer, Fik.
    The gladiators : history's most deadly sport / Fik Meijer.
        p. cm.
    ISBN 0-312-34874-6
    EAN 978-0-312-34874-8
    1. Gladiators. I. Title.

GV35.M45 2005
796'.0937—dc22   2005049380

First published in the Netherlands by
Atheneum – Polak & Van Gennep Amsterdam 2003.

First U.S. Edition: December 2005

10 9 8 7 6 5 4 3 2 1

'*Because, for such a long time now, ever since we sold our right to vote for nothing in return, the thought of continuing to allocate all the important posts in the state or the army the way we used to leaves us cold – no, people keep their heads down and ask for just two things: bread and circuses.*'[1]

Juvenal

Contents

List of Illustrations

Chronology

Introduction

It was a late afternoon in April. The bright sun was sinking behind the walls of the Colosseum, turning the golden light to pink. Seated high up in the amphitheatre, I was drifting into a daydream. How would I have behaved had I sat here for hours surrounded by 50,000 cheering and shouting Romans, while down in the arena the gladiators played a bloody game with death? Would I have enjoyed the slaughter, the horror, the stench of blood, the cruelty? Would I have let myself be carried away by the intense atmosphere, the screams and stamps, the applause thundering down into the arena from the galleries above, or would any feelings of excitement, exhilaration even, have been stifled by disgust at the cruel blood bath on show?

My daydream was interrupted by a portly tour guide, panting and heaving as he worked his way up towards me, a flock of tourists in his wake. He stopped close by to deliver a short history of the gladiator games in the Colosseum. He explained that here, down below us, there were ferocious sword fights, single combat to the death, literally thousands of people were crucified, or torn apart and gutted by wild animals. It was a well-researched account. But there was one question he failed to answer: a question put to him by one of his group. Why did the Romans have such a passion for the gladiator games? Why did they let themselves get carried away by such an orgy of bloodthirsty violence, time and again – over centuries? The guide could only come up with a few vague references to the appetites and instincts of the lower orders who had to be appeased with *panem et circenses*, 'bread and circuses', and to the power-hungry emperors who handled the situation so adroitly.

The group wandered on and I asked myself why the guide had been so vague on that one point. It was as if he did not want – or perhaps dare – to admit that the Romans had tremendous enthusiasm for gladiator games, that their popularity was utterly unprecedented: people talked about them every day in the bars and placed bets on fights.

We can hardly blame the tour guide. Even historians who have written in-depth studies on the subject wrestle with the phenomenon. Sometimes it almost seems as if they are angry with the Romans for perpetuating something so pernicious over so many centuries. History books describe the arena as a blood-soaked playing field where every sadistic impulse was given free rein, a place where Romans flaunted the very darkest aspects of their civilisation. To historians the games are scandalous, a monstrous phenomenon, a morass of hatred and sadomasochism. They regard gladiatorial combat, wild animal hunts, fights between men and animals, and the execution of condemned criminals in full view of a crowd stirred to fever pitch as the most debauched popular entertainment in history, and they invariably begin their accounts of the gladiator shows with expressions of their own personal disapproval. Some historians go to extremes. The most strident condemnation of all comes from Michael Grant, a British expert on the ancient world. Without a proper explanation and without offering any statistics or concrete comparisons, he writes in the introduction to his book *Gladiators* that the cruelties perpetrated in the arena were without parallel and that the shows in the Colosseum and other Roman amphitheatres were on a par with Nazi extermination procedures.[2] In his opinion, the atrocities of Genghis Khan were as nothing to what went on in the Colosseum. In other books, Jérôme Carcopino describes the Colosseum as a torture chamber and a human slaughterhouse,[3] while Georges Ville talks about 'the scandal of gladiator fights... an unthinkable monstrosity'[4] and J.P.V.D. Balsdon writes, 'No one can fail to be repelled by this aspect of callous, deep-seated sadism which pervaded Romans of all classes.'[5]

What all these historians have in common – and I could easily add to the list[6] – is their inability to explain satisfactorily how Roman culture could incorporate such excessive cruelties. In his book, Ugo Paoli makes a telling statement about the difficulties historians have in grappling with the issue: 'All this horrifies us... To say that we condemn this revolting custom is too little, we cannot even begin to understand.'[7] One consequence of their own physical revulsion at everything to do with the gladiator shows is that historians struggle to come up with a rational explanation as to how the phenomenon first arose. Plenty of attempts have been made, with very diverse results. Some believe that the gladiator shows stemmed from the Roman custom of human sacrifice. They believe the earliest gladiator games were part of a ritual to mark the death of a prominent citizen. Others view the games as an extension of the wars Rome engaged in. In this version, the events in the arena reflect the Romans' love of war and imperialism; wild animals and prisoners of war took part in victory parades for triumphant Roman generals and the purpose of gladiator fights was to commemorate the soldiers who had fought to establish Roman rule against all odds. By the time of the emperors, when huge military campaigns were no longer called for, the bloody battles in the arena had become a substitute. Others take the view that the fights in the arena served as a safety valve for ordinary people, the excitement of the slaughter alleviating the misery of their daily lives and the stresses they were exposed to. The emperors, who would leap at any opportunity to legitimise their rule, eagerly latched on to the idea, organising expensive shows as symbolic displays of power.

Present-day disapproval of the horrors of the arena is completely understandable, but we should not forget that our judgement springs primarily from our own norms and values. After a long, far-reaching process of civilisation, our social attitudes are rooted in criteria far removed from what the Romans thought of as respectable and appropriate. Using today's standards as a yardstick, it is easy to formulate a damning indictment of gladiator shows and the blood-lust they represented, embedded as they were in the value systems of a violent society. But how 'fairly' can we judge the phenomenon without studying it in its own cultural context? Ludwig Friedländer, the first scholar to make an exhaustive study of the gladiator games, writes:

Nothing indicates more clearly the enormous gulf between the people of ancient Rome and modern-day

Europeans in their sensitivities and ways of thinking than the different attitudes to the performances in the amphitheatre expressed by educated people then and now.[8]

A quick scan through the history books reveals just how recently public displays of violence like those in the arena were still going on in one form or another. It is true that from the fifth century onwards Christian literature features many critical and condescending references to the gladiator fights of ancient times, but single combat, which is what gladiator fights really were, did not disappear. One form in particular, the duel, emerged in various guises in mediaeval Europe. Of course there is a lot of difference between a duel and a spectacular gladiator fight, since duels were not actually advertised as popular entertainment, but the very nature of a duel – merciless single combat with deadly weapons – means it has a lot in common with the hand-to-hand fights in Roman arenas.

Closest of all to the ancient gladiator fights is the duel known as the judicial duel, which was seen as divine justice. It was literally a fight to the death. Two men accused of a crime would fight until one of them was dead. If the loser survived he would be killed at the end of the fight anyway, since defeat was seen as proof of his guilt. Another variant was the tournament duel. Although in this case the killing of one's opponent was not the main objective, many duels ended with the deaths of both combatants. From the late sixteenth century onwards, when these knightly duels were beginning to die out, a new type emerged, the formal duel, regarded by the participants as a formalised and ritualised form of permissible violence. Anyone who believed he had been insulted would challenge his opponent to settle the matter with a rapier, or in more recent times a pistol. Both parties were accompanied by seconds, whose job it was to convince the duellers, after they had succeeded in inflicting a number of sword or gunshot wounds, that they had done enough damage already. But the duellers often ignored them and carried on fighting. In France alone, no less than 8,000 aristocrats and officers met their deaths in this kind of duel between 1594 and 1610.

Public executions by order of the government, not unlike those laid on at lunchtime as part of the Roman gladiator shows, continued in Europe long after the collapse of the Roman Empire. Just like Roman emperors, the governments of mediaeval and early modern Europe displayed their power by holding public execution ceremonies. Far from evoking a sense of revulsion, the formal ritual used to demonstrate the state's monopoly on violence attracted large numbers of spectators. Like Britain, Holland was no exception. In seventeenth-century Amsterdam, a scaffold was erected on Dam Square as many as four times a year for the execution of serious offenders. It was not until the end of the eighteenth century that public executions ceased in Europe. In countries like Iran and China, executions are still held regularly in large stadiums, watched by thousands of spectators. In China, for example, no less than 1,700 people were publicly executed between April and June 2000. Two years later, sixty-four people were executed in one stadium in one day alone on Wednesday 28 June, for drug dealing. Until quite recently, the situation in Afghanistan was if anything even worse. As we k ow, there were numerous atrocities committed   that fragmented country 'on legal authority'. Both the troops of the   the n Alliance and the Taliban fighters committe ser s crimes against humanity. Neither side had any   as about hanging people in public, inflicting fatal r   dilations or chopping off hands and feet.

Cruel fights involving animals certainly did not come to an end when there was no longer any centralised Roman authority. Fights between men and animals went on in an organised way for a long time, both in the Byzantine Empire, which had replaced the Roman Empire in the east, and in the mediaeval states that had once made up the western part of the Roman Empire. People watched and were thrilled by them. There was a constant effort to think up novel ways of fighting with animals so that the public would not lose interest. In 1689, the authorities in Amsterdam felt obliged to announce an official ban on 'bear, bull or other fights with such creatures as dogs, bulldogs, pugs or dog-foxes in this city or within its jurisdiction'.[9] The ban did not stem from compassion for the poor animals but from government concern about public order. It would not be until the eighteenth century – well over 1,000 years later – that people began to condemn cruelty to animals and openly denounce the custom of torturing them.

The hunting and slaughter of wild animals, the main morning feature of a gladiator show, is still with us to this day. Every year, hundreds of thousands of people watch bullfights in Spain. No matter how gory the spectacle, no matter how many animals are killed and no matter how often things turn out badly for the *matadors*, *banderilleros* and *picadores*, people regard the graceful bullfighters as heroes. They dismiss any criticism on the grounds that this form of popular entertainment is rooted in a centuries-old tradition.

Although people generally disapprove of excessive displays of violence these days, we should not be complacent. In western society we still witness cruelties of a kind that that would not have seemed out of place in ancient Rome. Form and medium have changed, but untold cruelty is still with us. Bloody wars, revenge killings in the criminal underworld, street fighting, murder, torture and sadism – we have television programmes and films devoted to every one of them. How many violent films have been made in the past fifty years? Countless thousands. Not an hour passes without one of our many television channels showing a film in which violent homicide is a major element. Action films get bloodier all the time and there is no lack of avid consumers for cruelties of the kind seen in films by directors such as David Lynch and Quentin Tarantino.

Computer games broke the bounds of decency a long time ago. Blowing off heads has become so routine that it no longer disturbs us and the entertainment industry is doing very well out of it. Of course this is 'make-believe' rather than real violence. But on 25 April 2002, when a disturbed schoolboy in Erfurt, Germany, dressed in black like one of the lead characters in the computer game Counterstrike, emptied a handgun into his teachers, it seemed as if the line between fiction and reality had suddenly become very blurred. On such occasions, scientific studies are trotted out to demonstrate that in an average evening's viewing more than 100 murders will be shown on television. Yet a ban on all this violence seems inconceivable. The viewing and sales figures are simply too high. Even research indicating that on-screen violence leads to a long-term increase in violent conduct by young people fails to influence those who market the software. They produce their own research to show that computer games actually channel aggression.

Watching contact sports is popular too. People are prepared to get out of bed in the middle of the night to watch world championship heavyweight boxing. Each punch ratchets up the spectators' enthusiasm, especially if it leaves one man slumped against the ropes after taking so many blows to the head. A 'killer punch' is shown in minute detail, both at normal speed and in slow motion, and the pictures are broadcast all over the world. Objections from those who want to ban boxing are attentively listened to and then laid aside. Some boxers will stop at nothing to promote their sport. After Mike Tyson was knocked out in a challenge match against world champion Lennox Lewis on 8 June 2002, he said that for the same fee, more than 30 million dollars, he would be willing to fight a lion. He could model himself on Carpophorus, a man who floored an enormous lion in the Colosseum (see page 146).

It seems people are no less fascinated by violence today than the ancient Romans were. The triumphal march of Ridley Scott's film *Gladiator* is sufficient evidence of that. A piece of spectacle costing more than 100 million dollars, it became a box office hit, more because of the high degree of violence in the film than because of the tragic story of the life of Maximus, the main character, an army general who is relegated to the status of gladiator. Maximus, the 'good guy', is prepared to use any available means to further his crusade against the injustice he has suffered at the hands of 'bad guy' Emperor Commodus. He is only able to find peace by killing his hated opponent with his own hands.

The subject of this introduction is violence. I conclude with a story from the church father Augustine (AD 354–430), who lived at a time when gladiator fights were making a comeback. Although the shows had been reduced to a shadow of what they had once been, they could still pull tremendous crowds. There were people who simply could not resist going, including some who had publicly stated that they wanted nothing whatsoever to do with the games. In his *Confessions,* Augustine tells us what happened to Alypius, a very promising pupil of his, a boy from a good family in North Africa:

> After he had left for Rome ahead of me to study law, he somehow or other got carried away with an unaccountable enthusiasm for the gladiator games. This was especially odd because he detested that kind of thing and felt a deep loathing for the games. But when he happened to meet some of his friends and fellow students on their way back from lunch, they put subtle pressure on him and persuaded him, in spite of his initial firm refusal and resistance, to go with them to the amphitheatre on one of the days when the cruel games with death were being held there. Alypius said, 'Even if you drag my body to that place and sit me down, you won't be able to fix my spirit or my eyes on the games! So although present I will be absent, and by mastering the games I will master you!' His friends heard this, but they took him with them anyway, perhaps further encouraged to do

so by curiosity as to whether he could follow through on what he had said.

When they arrived they took some of the seats that were still free. The entire amphitheatre was already wild with gruesome exuberance. Alypius held the doors of his eyes firmly closed and forbade his spirit to come out and encounter something so wrong. If only he had blocked up his ears! Because at some turning point or other during the fight, startled by an enormous roar from the crowd, he allowed his curiosity to get the better of him. Thinking he was sufficiently prepared to cope with anything he might see, full of proud disdain, he opened his eyes and took a stab to the soul more forceful than the thrust taken in the side by the man he had opened his eyes to see, and he suffered a worse fall than the gladiator whose fall had prompted the roar from the crowd. That cry had penetrated his ears and unlocked his eyes, laying bare a place where he could be touched, so that his soul could be overthrown, a soul more foolhardy than strong, and all the weaker because he had placed his trust in himself instead of in You, as he ought to have done. Because along with the sight of blood he drank down a deep draught of inhumanity. He did not turn away, he continued to look, revelling in the wild frenzy without even realising it, feasting his eyes on that damnable fight and making himself drunk on bloody sensuality. And by that point he was no longer the man who had arrived at that place, but had become a true companion of those who had taken him there.

Why should I say more? He watched, he cheered, and in an instant he was alight with enthusiasm. When

11

he left that place he carried the infatuation with him and it would spur him to go back, not only with those who had taken him there the first time, but even ahead of them, taking other people with him.[10]

According to Augustine, eventually things did turn out right for Alypius, because ultimately he put his trust in God. But the story of Augustine's pupil illustrates how irresistible the attraction of the gladiator shows could be, even to people we might least expect to be receptive to it.

Central to this book is the idea that we are closer to the gladiator shows than we might like to admit. Many readers' impressions of gladiators will have been formed by films such as *Spartacus* and *Gladiator*. I want to give a clearer idea of what really happened, as far as we can tell from the reports of Greek and Roman writers, and artefacts such as ancient armour and weapons, as well as images that have come down to us in the form of mosaics, wall paintings and figurines. The centrepiece of the book is 'A Day at the Colosseum', where I have tried to imagine what a full day's programme from early morning to evening must have been like. To put this in context, I shall first describe how the gladiator shows developed over time and the backgrounds and fighting techniques of the gladiators themselves. I also give a picture of the Colosseum – that huge, amazing setting where these events took place – and explain how innumerable wild and exotic animals were transported to Rome year after year from North Africa and Asia. Gladiator fights were finally 'abolished' as I shall show, and in later centuries the Colosseum fell into decline. Finally, I cast a critical eye on the films *Spartacus* and *Gladiator*.

How the Gladiator Games Evolved

Throughout the first and second centuries AD, the gladiator show was an established part of Roman life. Almost every medium-sized town in the Roman Empire had an amphitheatre where games were regularly held, and people from all social classes came for the entertainment. Emperors publicised the shows and used them to demonstrate their solidarity with the people. Not only that, they used them to show that they had an almost unlimited degree of control over both people and animals. Given that gladiator games were so popular, it is surprising that Roman literature of the late republic and the imperial period mentions the actual origins of the games only three times, and even then very briefly. This may be because the gladiator fights had non-Roman origins – something the chauvinistic Romans preferred not to hear.

The most confident explanation of how the games originated is given by a Greek writer, Nicolas of Damascus, in the second half of the first century BC:

The Romans organised performances by gladiators, a habit they had acquired from the Etruscans, not only at festivals and in the theatres but also at feasts. That is to say, certain people would frequently invite their friends for a meal and other pleasant pastimes, but in addition there might be two or three pairs of gladiators. When everyone had had plenty to eat and drink, they called for the gladiators. The moment anyone's throat was cut, they clapped their hands with pleasure. And it sometimes even turned out that someone had specified in his will that the most beautiful women he had purchased were to fight each other, or someone else might have set down that two boys, his favourites, were to do so.[11]

The second account is by Isidorus of Seville in the seventh century AD. He wrote in his etymological dictionary *Origines*[12] that the Latin word *lanista*, meaning a gladiator manager or an agent trading in gladiators, was the word for 'executioner' or 'hangman' in Etruscan. And then there is the Christian author Tertullian, who lived in the late second and early third century AD. When Tertullian describes the way the strikingly dressed figure of Charon – a god of hell – entered the arena along with the god Mercury when the afternoon executions were over (and perhaps after gladiator fights as well), to accompany the bodies of the dead as they left the arena for the last time, his words instantly conjure up a picture of the hammer-swinging Etruscan god of death, also known as Charon (see page 159).[13]

Until the beginning of the twentieth century, almost everyone accepted the Etruscan theory. This was rather strange, to say the least, since in all the many Etruscan burial chambers that have been excavated, not a single depiction of an armed duel has ever been found, although there are pictures showing two men fist fighting. The closest thing to a gladiator is the figure of 'Phersu' in a mural in the Tomb of the Auguries at Tarquinia, which dates from the second half of the sixth

'Phersu' in a mural dating from the second half of the sixth
century BC in the Tomb of the Auguries, Tarquinia

century BC. It shows a masked, bearded man dressed in
a multicoloured shirt and cap and holding a dog or wild
cat on a leash while it attacks another man. Some
experts have explained this scene as a combination of
gladiatorial combat and a fight with wild animals, both
of which formed part of the all-day programme in the
imperial period. But however similar this image may be
to a hunting scene or to executions using wild animals,
to suggest that it represents an armed gladiator would
be very far-fetched.

The discovery in Lucania and Campania of grave
paintings which date from the middle of the fourth
century BC undermined the Etruscan theory. The
frescoes at Paestum illustrate various elements of the so-
called 'funeral games', among them a fight between two
armed men equipped with helmets, shields and spears.
The fact that there is an umpire in the picture suggests
that this must be single combat, in honour of an

15

Two combatants at funeral games fighting with spears,
lances and shields, in a mural at Paestum dating from the
first half of the fourth century BC

important figure who had died. Since the earliest known
references to Roman gladiator fights are to do with
contests staged at funerals, it seems most likely that the
custom came to Rome from Campania. But this does not
necessarily mean that the gladiator fights originated
there. It may well be that the Greeks, who were in this
region as long ago as the eighth century BC, introduced
their funeral games with human sacrifices to the area.
They believed that the blood of prisoners gave the dead
strength for the difficult journey to the underworld. It
could be that the funeral games in Campania slowly lost
any connection with their Greek roots, and human
sacrifices were gradually replaced by fights to the death
at the graveside.

The earliest Roman gladiator fights were part of
elaborate funeral rites for important people. Families
used them to ease the passage of a deceased relative

from the world of the living to the kingdom of the dead and at the same time to display their own affluence, status and power. Quite often the deceased aristocrat had left instructions about the programme of events, and his relatives simply carried out his final wishes. This explains why the funeral games were referred to as *munus* (plural *munera*), meaning a task that had to be performed, an obligation towards the dead person. The funeral games were a family affair, paid for privately out of the family's pockets to raise their social standing. They were organised without state involvement, even if the patrons were prominent figures, active in public life.

Tertullian was an apologist for Christianity[14] and he explains the significance of a series of gladiator fights that took place at the funeral of one prominent aristocrat. The ancient Romans believed they were performing a service to the dead by putting on these shows. Originally Roman funerals would have involved a much more cold-hearted kind of human sacrifice. Prisoners or less valuable slaves, bought solely for the purpose, would have been sacrificed in the conviction that the soul of the deceased would be cleansed by human blood. It is quite possible that Tertullian described Roman attitudes the way he did because he wanted to bring the gladiator fights into disrepute. On the other hand, Tertullian's explanation is also found in the earlier work of Festus, a second-century writer, who says quite simply:

It was the custom to sacrifice prisoners at the grave-sides of brave warriors; when the cruelty of this habit became known, they switched to gladiator fights beside the grave.[15]

The notion that gladiator fights were a soft substitute for human sacrifice is disputed by some scholars who fail to see the logic of the sacrifice connection.[16] They argue that the Greeks and Romans killed their sacrificial victims at funerals by cutting their throats on the funeral pyres of the deceased, or by burying them alive, but never invited them to take up a sword or a spear and attack someone else. So gladiator fights had nothing to do with human sacrifice. However, what I am suggesting is that by engaging in courageous duels during the funeral games, gladiators were meant to illustrate the virtues that had made Rome great, virtues demonstrated by the deceased himself during his lifetime: strength, courage and determination. Displaying these attributes in combat would help inspire young people to take the same path in life as their ancestors.

Chariot Races and Plays

When gladiator fights were first introduced to the Romans in the late fourth or early third century BC, two popular entertainments for the masses were already in full swing – these were chariot races and stage plays, which were performed during the *ludi*, public games organised by the state and financed by the treasury. The *ludi* and the gladiator games had very different origins. *Ludi* were held even in the early republic to celebrate special occasions marked by services of worship for a particular deity. Such festivals, which lasted just one day, were organised by the priests who served the particular deity to whom the games were dedicated. The two oldest festivals were the *Equirria* and the *Consualia*, both of which consisted entirely of horse racing. The

Equirria took place on 27 February and 14 March, in honour of the god Mars. The *Consualia* were held on 21 August and 15 December in honour of the god Consus, who was associated with Neptune, god of the sea and horses.

Under the Roman Empire (after 27 BC) more *ludi* were added to the calendar. The first games described in the records as lasting for more than one day are the *ludi Romani*, first mentioned by the historian Livy in connection with the events of 366 BC.[17] Tradition has it that these games were founded by one of the Etruscan kings of Rome, Tarquinius Priscus, in honour of Jupiter, Juno and Minerva, to commemorate the anniversary of the dedication of the Temple of Jupiter on the Capitol on 13 September. The event grew into a two-week festival, held from 4 to 19 September, with two main elements, the *ludi scaenici* (theatrical performances) and the *ludi circenses* (chariot races). More days were set aside for plays than for chariot races because races were a far more expensive form of entertainment. Sometimes the programme also included public banquets, military parades and competitive athletics.

By the first century BC the Roman calendar had even more fixed dates for *ludi*. The *ludi plebei* in honour of Jupiter were held every year from 4 to 17 November. The *ludi Apollinares* in honour of Apollo still took place from 6 to 13 July. Then there were the *ludi megalenses*, 4–10 April, in honour of Cybele, the mother goddess from Frygia. April could actually be described as a festival month, since the *ludi Cereales*, for Ceres, the goddess of fertility, took place from 12 to 19 April and 27 April was the first day of the *ludi Florales*, games held for the goddess Flora that lasted until 3 May. Sulla and Caesar, the

19

two dictators of the first century BC, established further *ludi* to commemorate their own successes. The *ludi victoriae Sullanae* ran from 26 October to 1 November and the *ludi victoriae Caesaris* from 20 to 30 July. By Emperor Augustus' reign, the number of days set aside for *ludi* had reached sixty-one, of which forty-eight were for theatrical events and the other thirteen for chariot races. And it did not end there. Emperor Marcus Aurelius (AD 161–180) cut the number of days for *ludi* to 135, so we are forced to conclude that in the preceding years there must have been even more than that.

Stage acts and chariot races were held in different places. Until the end of the republic, Rome had nothing comparable to the Greek theatres. In fact until 145 BC there was no suitable accommodation at all. From then on, most theatrical performances were held in the wooden theatre Lucius Memmius had presented to the city to commemorate his conquest of Greece the year before. It was 55 BC before Pompey had a real stone theatre built, the first in Rome. By doing so he was breaching a ban on the building of stone theatres for public entertainment. In 19 BC a second was added, Cornelius Balbus' theatre, followed six (or eight) years later by the great Theatre of Marcellus, substantial remains of which can still be seen today.

The theatrical performances on offer were far from sophisticated. It was mainly a matter of entertaining a large crowd, which meant making them laugh. Two theatrical genres were particularly suitable in this respect: the mime and the pantomime. The mime was a burlesque affair in which gesture was used to act out themes from everyday life. Themes such as adultery, falling in love, deviant sexuality, lying, deceit, homicide and murder were acted out on stage with considerable verve. From the way the audience reacted, the actors could tell whether their performances accorded with public taste. If the play failed to catch the mood, there would be uproar and the spectators would noisily leave the theatre long before the performance was over. In the late republic, pantomime began to compete with mime. In pantomime, the leading character was backed by a chorus and an orchestra and accompanied by a number of actors in supporting roles as he expressively depicted themes from mythology. This sometimes sent the audience into ecstasies as they sang along with the pantomime songs at the tops of their voices. Some songs became real hits, which did not please everyone. There were aristocrats who felt it had all got out of hand, that pantomime was terribly vulgar and that the actors, with their sometimes effeminate appearance, were an offence to traditional Roman values. Tacitus talks about the *licentia theatralis*, the licentiousness of audiences that allowed themselves to be carried away by the actors and behaved in an undisciplined manner.[18]

The leading actors in the other spectacle on offer at the *ludus*, the chariot races, could certainly not be accused of weakness or effeminacy. The charioteers were regarded as top-class athletes and regularly praised for their daring and skill. People in the crowd displayed fanatical support for their heroes and identified with them. When the chariot races were on, the atmosphere in the stadium was like that of a football stadium, except that the spectators were divided into four camps, not two. Each of the chariots in the race belonged to one of four *factiones*. These were stables with a large number of chariots and charioteers, each represented by one of

A relief dating from the first century AD showing a
four-horse chariot approaching the turning pillar

the four traditional colours. Before the race started,
every spectator knew exactly which colour
commanded his loyalty. You were a lifelong supporter of
the whites, the reds, the blues or the greens and crossing
over to a different stable was seen as treachery. Ordinary
people took sides most emphatically, but senators and
even emperors might also declare their lifelong loyalty
to one particular stable. Emperor Caligula was an ardent
supporter of the greens and often spent whole days at
the stables, dining with the charioteers.

The Circus Maximus was the fixed venue for chariot
races. It had been built in the valley between the Palatine
and Aventine Hills, on a stretch of flat ground 650 metres
long and over a hundred metres wide. It was traditionally

said to have been built by King Tarquinius Priscus and over the years it was adapted a number of times to the demands of the day. It was eventually able to hold a staggering number of people: more than 150,000. Originally there had been twelve races in a full day's programme but during the imperial period the number increased to twenty-four. There were hardly any breaks between races. The winner only just had time to accept his prize and do a lap of honour before the next chariots were drawn up to the starting line.

The procedure was always the same. The organiser used a flag to give the starting signal and the four-horse chariots (occasionally two- or three-horse chariots) belonging to the four stables shot away from their starting positions. The charioteers had to drive four times around the *spina*, the 344-metre long barrier down the middle of the Circus Maximus. The crowd could see how many circuits had been completed by the number of stone eggs, later marble dolphins, that clattered down in sequence above the *spina*. Needless to say, the charioteers ran tremendous risks during the almost 5-kilometre race, since there was a lot of jostling, especially on the bends. Serious or fatal injuries were common, but the organisers never had any reason to complain about a lack of charioteers, for the prize money was high. Many ordinary young men were willing to accept the risks in the hope of getting into the highest division, with its promise of fame and riches.

Gradually, from the second century BC onwards, a new event was introduced into the *ludi*, the hunting of wild animals (*venatio*). The first exotic creatures had appeared in Rome a century before. Simply exhibiting these animals had been enough to arouse huge enthusiasm. Animals taking part in parades and triumphal processions were seen as living proof of Roman dominion over unknown lands. In 275 BC, Curius Dentatus appeared leading several Indian elephants when he marched in a triumphal procession to celebrate his victory over Pyrrhus, King of Epirus. More than twenty years later, in 252 BC, Caecilius Metellus brought 142 elephants back to Rome after his victory over the Carthaginians in Sicily. They were floated across the Straits of Messina to mainland Italy on rafts made of transport amphorae lashed together, and then taken on to Rome. Pliny the Elder[19] tells us that some commentators claimed the elephants were slaughtered in the Circus Maximus because no one knew what to do with the enormous animals. Other sources claim they were not killed, but fail to tell us what did eventually happen to them.

When the initial astonishment had worn off, the Romans started looking for other forms of entertainment using wild animals in the arena, and arrived at the idea of the chase. The first proper hunt was staged in 186 BC during the *ludi* held by Fulvius Nobilior in honour of Jupiter. He had put together an extensive programme that included hunting lions and panthers.[20] Not everyone was happy with this development. Many senators objected, announcing quite openly that the *venatio* offended against traditional values. In 170 BC the senate even passed a law banning the import of wild beasts from Africa, although this was not motivated by a love of animals. The Romans' main concern was that Carthage, which was gradually recovering from the battering it had taken at the hands of the Romans during the Second Punic War (218–201

BC), might grow rich on its earnings from the trade in wild animals. The ban had little effect and the use of wild animals in the Circus Maximus continued as before. In 169 BC, the *aediles* Scipio Nasica and Cornelius Lentulus staged a spectacular hunting show with sixty-three unnamed African wild animals, forty bears and several elephants.[21] In 167 BC, Aemilius Paullus invented a new role for animals in the shows. He introduced a new sentence, *damnatio ad bestias*, death by wild animals. Deserters from the auxiliary forces (army units made up of non-citizens) were ripped apart by wild animals in the presence of large crowds. A feature of the games held by Scipio Aemilianus in 146 BC, it became an established part of the programme and was later also applied to slaves sentenced to death for committing serious crimes. In the last century of the republic there was hardly any significant protest at all against using wild animals during the games. Indeed, the more animals there were, the more the public enjoyed the shows.

Early Gladiator Fights

The first time gladiator fights are mentioned in Rome is in 264 BC, the year the First Punic War began.[22] The two sons of the ex-consul Iunius Brutus Pera arranged for three pairs of gladiators to fight each other at his funeral in the cattle market near Tiberine Island – the Forum Boarium. The fighters are called *bustuarii* in the sources, a word derived from *bustum*, meaning a funeral pyre or grave. This does not necessarily mean that the gladiators fought right next to the tomb of the deceased, only that their performances were part of a funeral ceremony. They probably fought some time after the burial had taken place, following a brief period of mourning.

Another fifty years have passed before gladiator fights are mentioned again. In 216 BC, the year the Romans suffered a humiliating defeat at the hands of the Carthaginians at Cannae, the three sons of the deceased ex-consul Aemilius Lepidus had forty-four gladiators (twenty-two pairs) perform at his funeral games.[23] This event took place in the Forum Romanum, the centre of Roman political power, chosen in preference to the old Forum Boarium because it offered more space. In 200 BC there were fifty gladiators at the funeral games held for Marcus Valerius Laevinus[24] and in 183 BC no less than 120.[25] A number of funeral games took place in 174 BC, the most memorable being those held by Titus Flamininus for his deceased father as part of a ceremony lasting four days, during which seventy-four pairs of gladiators fought each other.[26] In subsequent years the scale of the funeral games grew spectacularly. In 160 BC one incident demonstrated how popular they were. The premiere of the comedy *Hecyra* by Terence had drawn big crowds, but, in the middle of the performance, the audience left the theatre en masse and ran across to the Forum Romanum to watch the gladiator fights put on there by Aemilius Paullus.

In the course of the second century BC the Roman elite became steadily richer. Families devoted increasing amounts of time and money to gladiator fights in an effort to convince everyone that the deceased had belonged to the very highest class. The number of gladiators on the programme for each show started to run into the hundreds. Because the games had such a

Combatants at funeral games, probably *samnites*,
in a relief from a grave at Amiternum dating from the
middle of the first century BC

broad popular appeal, the direct connection between them and the funerals of dead ancestors started to fade. Aristocrats now regarded the funeral games principally as a way to increase their social standing, and began pandering to the public. A significant degree of opportunism was involved, certainly in the late republic. The senators, divided among themselves, had their eyes on their own careers and welcomed any opportunity to impress a wide variety of ordinary people. One event in 122 BC shows just how important the gladiator games were to anyone eager to curry favour with the public. Fights had been planned and a number of magistrates had arranged for stands to be built around the arena so that they could rent out seats. Gaius Gracchus, one of the people's tribunes that year, ordered that the stands be removed to give poorer people a chance to watch without paying. His demand was ignored, so he arranged for the staging to be dismantled the night before the performance so that free places could be offered the next day. The people responded with great enthusiasm, but his fellow tribunes were furious and this seems to have cost him his re-election as a tribune.[27]

In 65 BC, Julius Caesar wanted to hold gladiator fights for his long-deceased father, involving as many as 320 pairs of slaves. But the senate was afraid that Caesar, already very popular with the people of the city, would win even more followers, so it passed a law restricting the number of gladiators he could bring with him. This decision was mainly prompted by the fear that too many armed and well-trained fighters would arrive in a city with no official security force (a form of police force was introduced only under Augustus) and that, should a crisis develop, they might simply fall in behind their leader. Later, in 46 BC, when he had become a dictator and grown immensely wealthy from his victories in Gaul, Caesar no longer had to take much account of these kinds of sensitivities. When he organised gladiator fights in the Forum Romanum he used not only slaves, but also several Romans from respected families. There was one fight, Suetonius tells us, between Furius Leptinus, a man from a family that included a number of *praetors*, and Quintus Capenus, a lawyer who had once been a senator.[28]

The clear distinction between the *ludi*, which were organised by the authorities, and the *munera*, held by private individuals, remained until the middle of the first century BC. But the dividing line became increasingly blurred and it was only a matter of time before the magistrates started putting on gladiator games financed by the state. In April of 42 BC the moment finally arrived.[29] The political situation was particularly confused at this point and the sense of fear as to what the future might hold was overwhelming. A power struggle was now coming to a head between, on one side, Caesar's murderers Brutus and Cassius and, on the other, the supporters of the assassinated dictator. Some people believed that the Roman state itself was in danger, since strange omens were seen everywhere, pointing to great changes in the cosmos. In Rome the sun is said to have assumed enormous proportions and shone day and night, then to have collapsed in on itself giving hardly any light at all. The sound of trumpets and the clatter of weapons were heard from the direction of Caesar and Anthony's palace gardens in the middle of the night. People heard screams coming from army camps. A child was born with ten fingers on each hand and a mule gave birth to a foal that was a horse at the front and a mule at the back. The chariot of the goddess Minerva was smashed to pieces in the Circus Maximus and blood poured from the left shoulder of the statue of Jupiter in the Alban Hills. Rivers dried up or flowed back to their sources. The Romans regarded all these disturbances as a sign that the gods would have to be placated if the state was to be saved.

The *aediles* felt that the chariot races scheduled for the Circus Maximus as part of the *ludi Cereales* would not be enough to win the favour of the goddess Ceres, and they decided to organise gladiator fights instead. This decision was to have far-reaching consequences because until then gladiator fights had always been a private matter, bound up with the deaths of individual people. Now they were being used for a more elevated purpose: the continuity of the state. This meant that more money would be available for gladiator shows, allowing the programme to become broader and more varied. The hunting element of the *ludi* was transferred in its entirety to the gladiator shows.

Forum Romanum

Now only the facilities fell short. Although stone amphitheatres were being built in Southern Italy (see page 97) Rome still lacked an appropriate venue. Gladiator fights continued in the Forum Romanum or behind it on the Saepta Julia, a rectangular piece of fenced-off land where public meetings had been held in the time of the republic. The facilities had to be adapted before every show. Statilius Taurus made the first move to rectify this situation between 34 and 29 BC. He built a stone amphitheatre on the Campus Martius. It must have been less than impressive, because games were held in the Forum Romanum for several more decades.

Spartacus

As gladiator shows in the second century BC grew more prolific and spectacular, special gladiator schools were founded to train physically strong slaves under the supervision of gladiator managers (*lanistae*), and thus add extra panache to the funeral games organised by

Roman aristocrats. One of the oldest schools was situated in Capua, where Greeks, Macedonians, Thracians, Spaniards, Gauls and Syrians were trained to perform in the arena. According to our two most important sources, Plutarch and Florus,[30] the gladiator school at Capua was run very strictly by the gladiator manager Lentulus. The school administrators believe that the gladiators' diverse ethnic backgrounds m very unlikely they would offer any concerted res But their confidence proved misplaced. In 73 BC something happened that the Romans had completely failed to anticipate: eighty gladiators escaped. The escape plan has been attributed to three men, Spartacus, Crixus and Oenomaus. Little is known about the last two except that they were Gauls. Spartacus was a Thracian who had once served in the Roman army but deserted. He was caught by the Romans and sold as a slave, which was how he had ended up at the gladiator school in Capua. According to Plutarch he was not only extremely strong but also an intelligent and cultivated man, more like a Greek than a Thracian.

The rebels had only managed to take kitchen knives with them when they escaped, since the weapons they used in the arena were always very carefully stored out of their reach. Word of their escape soon reached the Roman authorities. Rome dispatched a detachment of soldiers against them. When army units arrived the rebels seized their weapons. Meanwhile Spartacus and his men had set up defensive positions on Mount Vesuvius, on difficult terrain. They used ropes made of vines to lower themselves through cracks in the crater into the deep interior of the volcano, then emerged from a well-concealed exit to mount a surprise attack on the Roman soldiers. This way they acquired yet more weapons, which they shared out among the plantation slaves who had joined them. The Romans still refused to recognise how disciplined an army this collection of disorderly slaves was, for they had been put through military training under the leadership of Spartacus and Crixus. So long as the Romans persisted in their ignorance, refusing to regard the escaped gladiators as worthy opponents, they would face losses and defeats. The tide only turned when they started deploying real armies against the rebels. Now the rebels' logistical disadvantages counted against them and it became clear that there were too few men among them with sufficient military experience to represent a long-term threat. Spartacus kept having to revise his objectives and he was unable to leave the Italian peninsular as intended. Eventually the rebels were surrounded at Bruttium, in the 'foot' of Italy, and defeated by an army led by Crassus. Spartacus fought bravely – as you would expect of a gladiator, says Florus – and met his death like a true army commander.

Nevertheless, the Roman magistrates had been given a serious fright. The government wanted at all costs to avoid a repeat performance, so control over the gladiator schools was strengthened. But members of the senate, wanting to back up political demands, had no qualms about hiring gladiators from the managers of training schools to serve in their private armies. In 63 BC, the Senate became frightened that Catilina, a senator who had twice been defeated in Consul elections, might employ armed gladiators to create a disturbance. A law was rushed through to ban the creation of armed units. The events of January 52 BC made it more obvious than ever that gladiators posed a threat to the established order. Two radical politicians, Clodius and Milo, were particularly active at the time. Gangs loyal to Clodius had already been in control of the streets of Rome for a considerable time and according to his political opponent Cicero there were gladiators among them. Milo built up an armed following in response. On 18 January Clodius marched along the Via Appia with a small body of men. Just outside Rome he was attacked by Milo, backed by a gang made up of 300 gladiators and an unknown number of armed slaves. Clodius was killed. This would be the last time gladiators were to play such a prominent role in a battle between private armies.

Gladiator Games under the Early Emperors

Emperor Augustus and his successors regarded the gladiator shows as good propaganda for the unity of the empire. In the imperial cities, the emperor cult and the gladiator games became increasingly bound up together. The priests of the emperor cult organised gladiator shows in honour of the living emperor. In Rome the emperors were personally involved in the shows, usually as impresarios, otherwise as keen spectators. The emperor had an effective monopoly on the games in Rome, because influential people with adequate financial resources were extremely hesitant about putting on shows themselves, aware that if the response to their games was too enthusiastic the emperor might become resentful. This was less of a concern in provincial towns, where not only priests of the emperor cult but ordinary citizens regularly stepped forward to organise shows, in the hope that their fellow citizens would appreciate their generosity.

Emperor Augustus (27 BC–AD 14) spared neither

expense nor effort, organising games for the people on a dazzling scale that had never been seen before. Shortly before he died he wrote in his political will and testament, known as *The Deeds of the Divine Augustus*:

> Three times I held gladiator games in my own name and five times in the name of my sons or grandsons. During the games, around 10,000 men fought each other to the death ... Twenty-six times I presented the people with hunting shows with wild animals from Africa, in the Circus Maximus or the Forum Romanum or the amphitheatre, either personally or on behalf of my sons or grandsons, and in them around 3,500 animals were killed.[31]

The extravaganzas staged by Augustus outstripped any of the shows put on by his predecessors in quantity, quality and variety, according to Suetonius.[32] Augustus could permit himself such enormous profligacy because by the time he had been in power for a few years his position had become virtually unassailable. To prevent rich senators from competing with him, he issued a decree in 22 BC limiting the number of gladiators other people were allowed to employ in their shows to 120, a small number compared to the tens of thousands he had used in only eight of his own shows. Everyone, like it or not, was forced to recognise that the gladiator games had become an imperial matter.

Augustus also decreed that gladiator fights should be held every year with fixed dates in December and March. Shows were to take place from 2 to 8 December and then from 17 to 23 December during the celebration of the *Saturnalia*, the carnival-style peace festival. Six to ten days in one month: clearly the Romans were not quick to tire of the fights. In spring the games ran from 19 to 23 March as part of the spring festival of *Quinquatrus*. The emperor was of course at liberty to add extra dates for games as the occasion arose, but it would have taken a very special occasion for him to treat the public to an additional show. It was not a matter of casually organising an extra event. The costs were far too high for that, even for an emperor. It was much cheaper to organise stage plays, or chariot racing. Philocalus' Calendar for AD 354 gives us a fair indication of the relationship between these three kinds of popular entertainment. Of the 176 registered feast days, 102 were reserved for theatrical events, sixty-four for chariot races and only ten for gladiator shows.

Augustus' successor Tiberius (AD 14-37) was a self-absorbed man with a tendency to depression, certainly not a fan of these extravagant events. He only occasionally came to watch and he was not at all interested in putting on any shows himself. He tightened the budget for the games and placed additional limits on the number of gladiators permitted to appear in events organised by others. Tiberius' aversion to gladiator fights was one of the reasons he was so unpopular: the people very nearly threw his body into the Tiber when he died (a tremendous insult). His lack of interest left room for speculators to organise games and to make substantial profits from ticket sales. In AD 27 in Fidena, a small town just to the north of Rome, this led to a real catastrophe. A certain Atilius, a freed slave, organised a show in a wooden amphitheatre. People came in their thousands, not only from Fidena and the surrounding districts but from Rome as well. Whether because of the poor construction of the amphitheatre or the size of the crowd, the packed stadium collapsed – outwards as well as inwards, according to Tacitus.[33] He writes that 50,000 people were killed or injured, among them not only spectators but people who happened to be near the amphitheatre at the time.

Under Caligula (AD 37–41) the gladiator games returned to centre stage. During the four years he spent subjecting the population of Rome to his capricious appetites, Caligula organised a number of shows in Rome and other Italian cities. The story goes that he also performed in the arena as a gladiator himself. It is not clear exactly where this happened, but it was probably not in Statilius Taurus' amphitheatre, since Caligula regarded it as unworthy of Rome. He preferred to organise shows on the Saepta Julia, behind the Forum Romanum, where he even intended to build a real amphitheatre. His successor Claudius had no enthusiasm for the idea and the plan was dropped.

Emperor Claudius (AD 41–54) was much cleverer. He realised that it was possible to pacify the Roman people only by giving them what they wanted. He jokingly called the citizens 'my masters' and, by making sure that the supply of grain was properly organised, guaranteed them a minimum of security. The same kind of thinking led him to put on gladiator shows, which he attended fanatically, seldom missing even the brutal executions at lunchtime. He also liked presenting the prizes and would occasionally join the hoi-poloi in counting on the fingers of their

North wall of the Colosseum

outstretched left hands as each gold piece was handed over to the winner.[34] He also loved large-scale theatrical events, and in AD 44 he re-enacted the storming of a British town on the Campus Martius, taking the lead role himself (see page 178).

The extravagant Nero (AD 54–68) held many gladiator shows. He spent a lot of time in the amphitheatre and thought up all kinds of novelties to attract more people to the games. He introduced women in the arena, an act with a Roman knight riding down a sloping tightrope seated on an elephant,[35] and mass fights between condemned prisoners. Like the equally insane Caligula, he thought that gladiator shows deserved more worthy surroundings than Statilius Taurus' theatre, so in AD 57 he had a wooden amphitheatre built near the Campus Martius. It never had a chance to establish a reputation, as it was reduced to ashes seven years later when Rome burned in AD 64.

In AD 70, Emperor Vespasian finally built an amphitheatre to match the greatness of Rome – surprisingly, since he had a reputation for thrift. He probably saw it as the perfect way to strengthen his ties with the people, justifying the enormous costs of construction. And so the Amphitheatrum Flavium arose, later known as the Colosseum. In AD 80 it was formally inaugurated with a show more spectacular than anything that had ever been seen before, attended by more than 50,000 people. If the gladiator games were not already popular, they became so now. The sources give the impression that the games were becoming steadily bigger and more expensive, with increasing numbers of gladiators and wild animals. The organisers did everything they could to thrill the public. They kept thinking up new events to add to the programme. They were determined to make a day at the Colosseum a talking point for years after the event.

The Gladiators

Gladiators came from all over the Roman Empire. Originally most of them were enemies defeated by the Romans in their wars of conquest, who had refused to recognise Roman authority, which meant that under Rome's dictatorship they forfeited their place in society. Most prisoners were either sold as slaves, executed, or forced to kill each other, but a few were sentenced to the gladiator school (*ludus*)[36] to be trained to fight in the arena. There they were joined by slaves charged with serious crimes and later by free men who had volunteered for their careers as gladiators. Once trained for their grand task, they set out to perform in front of a greedily expectant audience the way the Romans themselves had performed all over the world, in a life and death struggle.

Their Prestige

Given the backgrounds of most gladiators, it is hardly surprising that Roman aristocrats ranked them at the bottom of the social scale. To the patricians the gladiator was a rough, frightening outsider, a doomed man beyond hope of reprieve, an utterly disreputable slave. But even those who described gladiators as low, contemptible beings could not deny that, in the arena, they behaved with dignity, and showed a resolute demeanour in the face of death, so a degree of ambiguity crept into the verdict, a mixture of disdain and admiration. This is how Cicero, who repeatedly reviled his political opponents, Clodius and Marcus Antonius, by calling them gladiators, described his own ambivalent attitude:

> Down-and-outs or barbarians they may be, but just like well-brought up men, they'd rather take a hit than dodge away in cowardly fashion. Look at how often their main concern seems to be to court the approval of either their master or the people. Even when covered in wounds, they will send someone to their master to ask what he wants of them. If he feels they have done enough, they are prepared to die. What gladiator of even the most mediocre calibre has ever groaned, or so much as winced? Which of them has ever disgraced himself by failing to move, let alone by giving in? Which of them has ever pulled his head in after submitting and hearing the coup de grâce announced? Such is the power of training, preparation and practice.[37]

Seneca, a stoic, goes even further. He presents the brave gladiator as an example to the wise man. The gladiator, bound by his oath, places his life in the hands of his master, just as the wise man must surrender his life to his divine master. To the gladiator, with his low social standing, the arena was the one place where he could find fame and honour and display his bravery, his *virtus*. Seneca does not think gladiators should be pitied. It was no less true for other sectors of society that fame and honour could only be acquired through great effort,

Bronze figurine of a surrendering *thraex*, dating from the
first century AD

pain, and ultimately death.[38] There is no room for pity in
Seneca's view of the matter.

To the Christian author Tertullian, a self-declared
opponent of the gladiator shows, the conflicting
emotions displayed by the Romans were grist to the mill.
He writes:

During one and the same performance they sing their praises and humiliate and belittle them. They condemn them to public disgrace and to the loss of their rights as citizens. They exclude them from the senate and ban them from the tribunes and from the ranks of senators and knights. They deny them any honour or distinction... But at the same time they love those they punish and disparage those they respect. They hold the skill itself in high regard but despise the man who displays it. What kind of judgement is this, that a man deserves commendation for the very same reasons that he inspires contempt?[39]

Tertullian was right. Gladiators were regarded as slaves who had been condemned to death, as men unworthy of any respect, yet at the same time they were seen as possessing the traditional Roman virtues of strength and courage (*fortitudo*), discipline and training (*disciplina*), tenacity (*constantia*), stamina (*patientia*), fearlessness in the face of death (*contemptus mortis*), desire for fame (*amor gloriae*) and the will to win (*cupido victoriae*). These are precisely the virtues that would have reminded audiences of the soldiers who had made Rome famous all over the world. Of course there were gladiators who did not fit this idealised image, who were afraid and tried to avoid the fight. This made them once again the lowest of the low, outsiders who deserved to die in the most humiliating way.

Their Backgrounds

From the first century BC onwards, it was not just prisoners of war who were condemned to the status of gladiator but an increasing number of slaves as well. Any slave who had committed a grievous offence (murder, poisoning, or desecration of the temple) ran the risk of being sentenced *ad ludum gladiatorium* (to the gladiator school). In the long run this amounted to a death sentence, although the condemned man was offered a chance of rehabilitation. He could literally fight his way back into society by coming up with a performance that satisfied the crowd. A slave who was condemned *ad bestias* (to death by wild animals) or a citizen whose sentence was *ad gladium* (death by the sword) was a lot worse off. He knew that a gruesome end awaited him. Slaves sentenced to die on the cross (*crucifixio*) faced an even more harrowing death, since the end was agonisingly slow.

Although the arena was the province of ignominious prisoners of war and slaves, free men also became so captivated by the atmosphere and the excitement that they voluntarily reported to one of the gladiator schools and signed a contract for a specific period. It must have been primarily the excitement and the potential winnings that persuaded them to give up their status as free men, in some cases even Roman citizens, and to opt for a life among condemned slaves under a gladiator boss. Sometimes they had a special reason for aspiring to the life of a gladiator. A Scythian called Sisinnes, for example, joined a gladiator school in Amastris on the Black Sea coast of his own free will in the hope that his fights would earn him the total of 10,000 drachmas he needed to buy a friend's freedom.[40] Many were motivated by the prospect of escaping poverty. Where they were unemployed or underemployed and strug-gling to provide for their own basic needs, life as a gladiator offered security. If they became gladiators they would at least be well provided for and might even be able to improve their financial position. Volunteers were often ex-soldiers who had not been averse to violence during military service and after leaving the army had found it hard to adapt to the monotony of civilian life. In the gladiator school they became members of a community that put the military virtues of bravery, daring and loyalty into practice in the arena.

We have no way of knowing the relative numbers of prisoners of war, condemned slaves and free men who went through this process. All we can say is that in the late republic the vast majority of gladiators were prisoners of war and slaves, but in the first century AD the number of volunteers joining them steadily increased. Based on grave inscriptions alone, it seems as if the two groups were roughly equal in size, except that gladiators who were able to immortalise their names in an epitaph would generally have been the successful ones, including a few who were set free after a stay of several years in a gladiator school, or who had bought their freedom with money they had earned. Most gladiators who died young could not pay for epitaphs, so they remain nameless. It seems, too, that there were more free gladiators in the provinces, particularly in the Greek-speaking ones, than in Rome.[41]

Even the sons of senators and knights volunteered. Most of them did not go beyond an appearance with wooden training weapons. Only a very small number risked their necks in a fight with 'battle-ready weapons'. Perhaps for these men it was more than simply a question of excitement and the chance of gaining widespread popularity. Other motives may have been involved:

perhaps they wanted a radical change of life. They may have become the black sheep of their families, made some kind of rash decision or run into financial problems. The arena was their last resort. You could compare them to those nineteenth- and twentieth-century aristocrats, down on their luck, who enlisted in the French Foreign Legion. Like them, the Roman aristocrats were opting for oblivion, for a life in which their present status would cease to hold any significance. They shared their lives with the urban proletariat and slaves, people they may have regarded until then as unworthy of so much as a glance.

There were also some foolhardy aristocrats who wanted to appear in the arena without having to go through a long period of training at the gladiator school. They regarded sword fighting as simply a good way of passing the time. Undeterred by criticism from their peers, they fought with people who had become social outcasts. In 46 BC during the great show held for Caesar in the Forum Romanum, the combatants included Furius Leptinus, the son of a *praetor*, and Quintus Capenus, a former senator and lawyer.[42] Several times from 38 BC onwards the senate tried to dissuade senators and knights from entering the arena, arguing that it was incompatible with their honour and status, and a threat to the senate's reputation. It is doubtful whether this had much effect: only a few years later the senator Quintus Vitellius fought in a show put on by Octavian, at the dedication of the temple to his deified father Caesar,[43] and in AD 11 this same Octavian, by then an absolute monarch who had been awarded the title *Augustus* (the exalted), gave Roman knights permission to fight in the arena.[44] Emperor Tiberius tried to introduce a ban immediately on his accession to the throne, but apparently with little success,

45

since in AD 15 two knights fought in a gladiator show held by Drusus and Germanicus.[45]

The senators and knights who entered the arena knew that they were exposing themselves to the scorn of their peers, but they endured all the derision and sometimes even revelled in it publicly. There were various levels of voluntary self-humiliation among members of the elite. Most of them kept the scandal within bounds by fighting as traditional gladiators in helmets that completely covered their heads so that they were less easy to recognise. But a certain Gracchus, an aristocrat about whom nothing else is known, chose to enter the arena as a *retiarius* (see page 90) with his head bare. Juvenal describes this ignominious performance:

> Gracchus, scorn of the city, who enters the fight
> Without weapons, without a shield or Thracian sword,
> Not wanting them, hating those accoutrements,
> Doesn't even don a helmet.
> No, first he throws his trap-net
> Unsuccessfully, and with a trembling hand,
> And pokes his trident out ahead of him,
> Then he turns his naked gaze toward the tribunes
> And flees this way and that, in front of everyone!
> Even Gracchus' opponent feels the shame of it
> More painfully than any wound.[46]

The opposite sometimes happened too. Capricious emperors might deliberately choose to humiliate certain senators and knights by forcing them to take up the gladiator's sword. At one point Caligula decided that a certain knight had insulted his mother Agrippina, so he sent him into the arena. When the man emerged from the fight victorious he was handed over to the executioners and killed anyway, contrary to all the rules and regulations, along with his father, who had nothing whatsoever to do with the affair. In another incident he demanded that a man fulfil his promise to perform as a gladiator if the emperor recovered from a serious illness. He only let him go when the man had succeeded in winning the fight and had begged for mercy several times. Nero went to even greater extremes. Apparently he once made 400 senators and 600 knights perform as gladiators, including some highly respected men with unblemished reputations. He went on to humiliate them even more by deploying them as hunters of wild animals (*venatores*) and using them to staff the arena.

Sometimes even the emperor could not resist the arena's lure. An appearance by the emperor must, of course, have involved elaborate safety precautions to minimise his chances of being injured. Caligula, Titus, Hadrian, Lucius Verus (dual emperor along with Marcus Aurelius) and Didius Julianus (who was emperor for several months in AD 193) were more than prepared to fight as gladiators. Whether their performances were one-off events or whether they entered the arena on a regular basis is unclear. We do know that the most notorious emperor in this regard, Commodus, regularly dressed up as a gladiator, using the name Hercules the Hunter. The association with Hercules was well chosen, since he was a god very popular with both gladiators and the public. Cassius Dio, who claims to have attended a number of this emperor's fights, gives a less than flattering impression of his exploits. He calls the emperor's gladiatorial hobby 'a little game'.[47] No gladiator would dare to inflict real wounds on an emperor.

Commodus holding a club and wearing a lion's head cape

Commodus' act must sometimes have made him look quite ridiculous. One day he stood in the arena and turned towards the senators in the audience with the severed head of an ostrich in one hand and a sword in the other.[48] Whether the implied threat was a 'joke' or in deadly earnest is difficult to say. On another occasion he shot dead 100 bears, not from within the arena as was the usual practice but from the balustrade. This was no great challenge, since the arena had been divided in four with walls set at right angles so that the bears, separated into four groups, were hemmed in on all sides. When he grew tired halfway through the slaughter and a woman passed him a chalice of wine, he drank it down in one, while the people and the senators (no doubt by order of the authorities) shouted, 'May you live a long life'. He killed panthers and lions from a raised platform too. The writer Herodianus does add in an aside that he was rarely seen to use a second spear because the first throw almost always hit its target. Once, when a panther had knocked down the servant responsible for letting it out of its cage and was about to maul him, Commodus jumped in first with his spear and inflicted a deadly wound on the animal. He did go down into the arena to run after deer and gazelles. He chased them and killed them with well-aimed throws. Although there were doubts about his intellectual faculties and his courage, his accuracy was never in question.[49]

We do not know whether he made an impressive gladiator, although the applause from the audience must have convinced him time and again that he had produced a really first-rate performance. He selected his own opponents and they were not renowned fighters but members of the audience who had no combat experience at all and who must have been on the defensive even if they did, since they regarded him as an emperor, not as a gladiator. They were often armed only with wooden swords. On one occasion Commodus went to such lengths that it must have disgusted everyone. He ordered all the people who had lost their left foot as the result of disease or an accident to be gathered together in the arena. They were given sponges instead of rocks to defend themselves with. He flogged them all to death with a stick and made it look as if he were killing giants, just like Hercules. He had himself royally rewarded for this performance – 1 million *sestertii*.

Commodus was hugely jealous of gladiators who were skilled at handling weapons. This jealousy cost one man his life. He had chased a lion around the arena on horseback and finally killed it, which was seen as a remarkable feat. Commodus could not stand the fact that this gladiator had become so overwhelmingly popular, so he had him killed.[50]

Septimus Severus, who was also a devotee of gladiator shows, might have liked to enter the arena but had to relinquish this ambition because he had weak feet. He reproached the senators, saying that the *damnatio memoriae* (the posthumous condemnation of an emperor), proclaimed in the case of Commodus partly on the grounds that he had repeatedly fought in the arena, was sheer hypocrisy on their part. He snapped at them:

> You say Commodus fought as a gladiator. Don't any of you fight as gladiators? If you don't, why have some of you bought shields and those famous gold helmets?[51]

Their Training

Anyone sentenced to the gladiator school became part

of the *familia gladiatoria*. As an individual he now came second to the prestige of the school and had to give up any notion of privacy. He swore a solemn oath (*sacramentum*) officially confirming his downgrading, promising to endure the worst kinds of humiliation and to suffer death by fire, in chains, or by the sword without protest. With this oath the gladiator dedicated himself to the gods of the underworld, on whose orders his life would be either spared or sacrificed. This is not unlike the vow made by the Roman general Publius Decius Mus, who before a decisive battle in 340 BC promised that he would not seek to avoid death at the hands of his enemies. This promise was part of a declaration in which he dedicated himself to the gods of the underworld. The difference was that gladiators did not take their oath willingly but under duress. In return they would not be handed over to an executioner and lose their lives in the most dishonourable way possible.

Before taking the gladiator's oath, men who became gladiators of their own free will signed an agreement (*auctoramentum*) with a gladiator manager, stating that they were contractually obliged to perform as gladiators for a given period. This contract stated how much they would earn as well as how often they would fight and with which weapons. Some of these men would have been ex-gladiators who had re-applied after being freed, in the hope of creating a reasonable life for themselves with the prize money they might earn.

Once accepted into the gladiator family, the recruit entered another world where the standards and laws of normal society did not apply, only the rules of the barracks. He was now the property of the gladiator manager, who took charge of his training and hired him out to the people who organised tournaments. From this point onwards, his life was spent largely within the walls of his school. He trained day in, day out, on the rectangular training ground. He lived in barracks, in a tiny cell of no more than 3 by 4 metres, often without windows, on one of the longer sides of the training ground. He took his meals with the other gladiators in a big canteen on one of the shorter sides of the ground, next to the hospital where he could be treated if necessary. His weapons were stored in a special armoury, securely guarded by watchmen whose job it was to ensure that he never had an opportunity to get hold of weapons after a day's training and create any kind of disturbance.

The gladiator school at Pompeii

There is no way of knowing how many gladiator schools there were in the whole of the Roman Empire, but to judge by the number of cities with relatively large amphitheatres (see List of Amphitheatres), there must have been more than a hundred. Some schools, such as those at Nîmes, Arles and Pergamum, had good reputations and offered accommodation to trainers and gladiators from Italy who arrived there on tour. Most schools were in the hands of independent gladiator managers. The gladiator manager was not only the head of the school but also an agent who dealt in gladiators. He bought, sold and hired out his pupils, preferably to one of the four schools in Rome. These were not headed by independent gladiator managers but by imperial functionaries (*procuratores*), who were responsible for running them and who also offered advice to the organisers of shows when it came to taking on gladiators. Because of the importance of the job, they were only appointed after a meticulous selection procedure within the patrician class. They were extremely well paid. The director of the most important school, the *ludus magnus*, received an annual salary of 200,000 *sestertii*, making him one of the best paid civil servants in the entire imperial bureaucracy. One reason for this may have been that his job was not entirely without its risks. Well-trained gladiators lived in these schools and there was always the fear that a spark of protest could ignite the school and that the gladiators could suddenly present a threat to public order, just as Spartacus had. That was something the emperors wanted to avoid at all costs, which was why they entrusted the running of these schools to heavyweight characters.

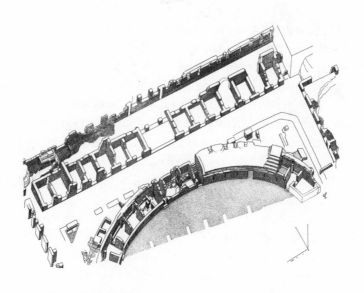

Three-dimensional representation of the remains of the
ludus magnus behind the Colosseum, showing one end of
the arena and the barracks that housed the gladiators
(drawing by Filippo Coarelli)

The four schools in Rome were all near the
Colosseum. From a surviving fragment of the Forma
Urbis, a marble map of Rome dating from the time of
Septimius Severus (AD 193–211), and from excavation
work between Via Labicana and Via San Giovanni 100
metres to the north-east of the Colosseum, we have a
reasonably reliable idea of the layout of the most
important school, the *ludus magnus*. It was a well-
equipped training complex with a large training ground,
tiers of seating, and barracks for the gladiators. The
training ground was in fact a small arena with the
characteristic elliptical shape, 62 metres long and 45
metres across. On the long sides, 'ordinary people' could

attend training sessions and on the short sides people in authority would sit in their own boxes, sometimes including the emperor himself. Along the northern side stood the cells that housed the gladiators, fourteen of which have survived reasonably intact. They are about 4 by 5 metres in floor area and each one probably housed two gladiators. No traces of beds have been found; the gladiators probably slept on simple army bed frames. The school was directly connected to the Colosseum by a passageway leading to the catacombs. The *ludus dacicus* and the *ludus gallicus* clearly had less elevated reputations. They had originally been training institutes for Dacian and Gallic prisoners of war. Later this ethnic distinction ceased to apply. The *ludus matutinus* was mainly used to train fighters destined to take on wild animals: the *venatores* (hunters) and the *bestiarii* (men who fought wild beasts).

Every school had strict entry requirements. When an aspiring gladiator – the Roman term for him was *novicius* – walked in through the main gate of the barracks, he was first examined by a doctor, who paid particular attention to his physical appearance. The school rejected any obviously unsuitable candidate either because he would be unable to withstand the harsh training programme or because he was unattractive. *Novicii* who passed this inspection procedure were tested again at intervals throughout their training, especially if they had suffered a serious injury in a fight. A gladiator who had lost much of his physical appeal would be removed from the school, since nothing was worse than a combatant attracting pity from the crowd during a serious fight.

For as long as a gladiator was attached to a school he

received medical attention. After all, a gladiator manager had put money into his training and did not want to lose his investment. The athletes were attended to by capable doctors, among them perhaps the best known doctor in the history of Rome, Galen. Before becoming personal physician to Emperor Marcus Aurelius he was employed for several years at a gladiator school in Pergamum. In his medical treatises, where he often draws on his experiences at the school, he insists that good medical care is essential, since only athletes in peak condition can produce fights that will appeal to the public. A good diet* was also essential, although in his opinion this was sometimes lacking. The everyday menu often included a kind of barley gruel with beans, which even earned the gladiators a nickname, *hordearii*, barley-porridge-eaters. Galen did not really approve of this diet, since it made gladiators too fat and flabby, but he had to admit that it gave them one advantage – their 'fatty layer' afforded them some protection against minor wounds.[52]

From the start, gladiator recruits (*tirones*) were taken in hand by special trainers (*doctores*). These were usually ex-gladiators who had survived many fights and were no longer in a fit state to appear in the arena themselves because of wounds or advanced age. The gladiator manager determined which recruit would be trained with which weapon and then entrusted him to a specialist, who would work him to the limits of his strength, using the same exercises for days on end to ingrain automatic responses, turning him into a veritable fighting machine.

Right from the start there was competition within the group and a hierarchy quickly emerged. Rivalry was rife even during the first exercises with wooden weapons against a two-metre pole (*palus*) and it became all the more fierce once the gladiators started to engage in real fights. Anyone who had survived his first fight could call himself *veteranus*. He spent the rest of his career trying to get to the top. The best combatants were given the title *primus palus* (first pole), the group below them *secundus palus* and so on. Veterans with many victories to their name were trying to maintain the existing order of merit and this gave them a psychological advantage in fights. A gladiator of a lower rank would think twice before taking the initiative and frantically throwing himself into a life-and-death struggle with a renowned opponent.

We should not underestimate the training gladiators went through, which we can glimpse from advice given by a fourth-century writer, Vegetius. At the time he was writing, the traditional discipline of the Roman armies was at rock bottom. To encourage his emperor – probably Theodosius I (AD 379–395) – he wrote a work entitled *The Military Institutions of the Romans* in which he pays a lot of attention to the ideal training for legionaries. It is clear that the demands Vegetius believes should be placed on soldiers also apply to aspiring gladiators:

The ancients, the books tell us, trained recruits in the following manner. They made round shields from willow branches, woven in the same way as baskets. This basketwork weighed twice as much as an ordinary shield. Instead of swords the recruits had fencing sticks which were also twice the usual weight. Equipped in this way, the new soldiers practised against poles, morning and afternoon. Training at the pole is not only good for soldiers, gladiators benefit from it too. In the arena or on the battlefield, only those who can be said to have prepared themselves thoroughly at the pole have the stamp of invincibility when armed. Each recruit planted his own pole so that it stood firm and rigid and stuck six feet out of the ground. Using the pole as if it were an opponent, the recruit practised with his basketwork shield and his club instead of his sword and his real shield. One moment he would make a frontal assault high up on the pole, as if attacking the head and face, the next he threatened the flanks, then attempted to wound the knees or lower legs, then pulled back, moved forward, leapt up and threw himself at the pole using all possible means of attack and all the tactics of war, as if it were a real enemy. This method of training involved making sure the recruit could draw himself up to inflict injury without exposing any part of his own body to a blow from the enemy.

Recruits also learnt that they should not slash with the edge of the sword but stab with the point... A cut, no matter how powerfully inflicted, is rarely fatal because the vital organs are protected by both weapons and bones, whereas a stab wound two thumbs deep is deadly, because any thrust that enters the body is bound to hit the vital organs. Furthermore, reaching back to strike a blow exposes the right arm and side, whereas with a stabbing action the body remains covered. The opponent is wounded before he even realises it.[53]

Their Life Expectancy

The daily life of a gladiator involved a real inner conflict. Inevitably some must have found it difficult having to train during the day with fellow gladiators they might be forced to kill a few days later in order to survive themselves. How did the conversation go when a gladiator sat down to his evening meal opposite someone he knew well, someone he got along with, who would nevertheless shortly become his opponent in life-and-death combat? The fact that, like craftsmen, gladiators formed their own unions (*collegia*) is an even more dispiriting thought. There were regular meetings, members placed themselves under the protection of a god or goddess for whom they held services of worship, and they made sure that any gladiator who died was given an appropriate funeral. So it was perfectly possible that a gladiator who was responsible for the death of a fellow gladiator might mourn at his graveside along with other members of the union. A grave inscription from the end of the second century[54] tells us a bit about how one such trade union was organised, in this case under the protection of the god Silvanus. The members were divided into groups of ten (*decuriae*). The 'top group' consisted of the best fighters, irrespective of the weapons they fought with, the second group, led by an experienced gladiator, was made up of the rather less successful fighters, and in group three were the recruits who had yet to perform officially.[55]

Living conditions were not always easy, especially for gladiators who did not make a great name for themselves but remained marginal fighters. New recruits who could not cope with the strict discipline must sometimes have despaired and tried to escape, though the guards were always on the *qui-vive*, and would take preventive measures. Potential escapees had their feet clamped to brackets and were permanently guarded. Gladiators whose performances were mediocre were not much better off. They did have some freedom of movement but they missed out on the bonuses received by their more successful fellow fighters and there was no way they could relax in anticipation of the next fight; they lived in a state of constant stress, dreading the prospect of dying a dishonourable death in the arena. Sometimes they were so fearful of this that they chose to end their lives themselves. In one of his letters[56] Seneca tells the sad story of a German who was assigned to the *bestiarii*. Before he was sent into the arena he went to the lavatory, the only place where he could separate himself off from the rest without being watched by the guards. He took the stick with a sponge at one end that was used for wiping the buttocks and drove it with great force into his throat. He died of suffocation. In the same letter Seneca describes another suicide. A despairing barbarian, a prisoner who was meant to perform in a *naumachia* (see page 176), took his own life by driving a spear into his own body. His last words were:

> Why oh why did I not escape long ago from these torments and taunts? Why should I arm myself to wait for my approaching death?

That the suicides Seneca writes about in this letter were no exception is clear from the work of the Roman orator and politician Symmachus (fourth century) who said that twenty of the gladiators he had intended to use in one of his shows had committed collective suicide. While waiting to be called they killed each other, leaving the audience thoroughly perplexed.[57]

Gladiators knew that their chances of ending their careers in good health and becoming trainers, or of going on to exercise another profession in civilian life were slight. A fight could end in one of five ways: a gladiator could emerge victorious; he could be killed fighting; he could be killed after capitulating by order of the emperor and the people; he could be shown mercy and be allowed to leave the arena alive after all; or he might be allowed to leave along with his opponent after a fight that had ended in a draw. On the basis of thirty-two fights that took place in the first century, in which six of the sixty-four gladiators were killed, the French historian Georges Ville concludes that of 200 gladiators taking part in 100 fights, nineteen were likely to die as a result. This would mean that at the start of a fight each gladiator had a 10 per cent chance of being killed. For the loser the chances were around 25 per cent and it is not known how many of these succumbed to their wounds during or after the fight, nor how many were reprieved. In subsequent centuries the loser's chances of survival declined. All the evidence suggests that there was a hardening of attitudes and that both the emperor and the general public wanted to see more blood. A defeated gladiator would only be allowed to leave the arena if the spectators were convinced he had behaved heroically. Ville estimates the average chances of survival for a third-century gladiator at 3:1. The loser had a fifty-fifty chance of emerging with his life.[58] Just how grim these fights could be is clear from the number of dead gladiators depicted in the floor mosaics in the Galleria Borghese in Rome, which date from the fourth century AD. The sections that have been preserved show nine freshly killed gladiators and eight winners. These images probably represent a gladiator show *sine missione*: the defeated gladiators would not be shown mercy (see pages 64-5).

Relief on the grave of a *retiarius* recording the various
fights he won in the course of his career

For some gladiators the end came early. The grave inscription of one young man from Padua shows that he died at the age of twenty-one. He had spent four years in a gladiator school and in all that time he had officially seen action on only five occasions.[59] This low number seems surprising. Surely a gladiator manager would at least want to recover his investment by deploying a man more often than that? But presumably the trainer only 'put him up' officially when he was sure that the young gladiator could offer the audience value for money. The grave inscription does not mention anything of the kind, of course, any more than the texts on the graves of other gladiators who died young indicate what the manager was planning for them.

Most gladiators died between the ages of twenty and thirty with between five and thirty-four fights to their name. There were some gladiators, however, for whom it was all over after only two or three appearances, as is clear from an inscription at Venusia in Italy, written to commemorate the *lanista* Gaius Salvius Capito. In the part of the text that is still legible, nineteen members of his school are named. There are numbers next to their names, which probably refer to the number of fights they had taken part in: three gladiators had seen action only once, four men twice, three men three times, one man four times, two men five times, one man six times, two men seven times and three men twelve times.[60]

One thing the inscription does not mention is the time span within which all these fights took place. I think two or three fights a year would be a reasonable estimate, given that a gladiator needed time to recover from his wounds and the audience might grow tired of watching the same fighters too often. On the other hand some gladiators did perform in the same arena very frequently

One of the fifth-century mosaics in the Galleria Borghese
showing fights to the death

indeed within a short period. During Emperor Trajan's nine-day show, one gladiator fought every day. The emperor and the crowd were suitably appreciative and gave him his freedom when the games were over.[61]

Gladiators aged over thirty are in a small minority. They must have been the regular winners, and they must also have had the good fortune to be shown mercy when they did lose because the spectators consistently felt they had defended themselves bravely and did not deserve to be killed. In Sicily a grave inscription has been found of a gladiator who died at the age of thirty after thirty-four fights: he had won twenty-one of them,

nine fights had ended in a draw and he had lost four times, saved on those occasions only by the intervention of the organiser and the spectators.[62] This kind of appeal for mercy is easy to understand. Precisely because the organisers did all they could to arrange for gladiators of comparable strength to fight each other, it was in no one's interests to see a fighter renowned for always fighting back with all his strength killed at the behest of the crowd. This probably explains why some gladiators were active in the arena until an advanced age, even when they were well past forty. Some were unable to resist and simply went on fighting, including Flavius Sigerus of Caesarea in Mauretania, who died at the age of sixty and who arranged for his gravestone to state that, not long before, when he retired, he had been awarded the sword of honour to show that he had rounded off a glittering career and lived as a free man from then on.[63] Flavius Sigerus probably belongs to that select group of successful gladiators who had many dozens of victories to their name. Others who belong in this category are Auctus with fifty victories, Nasica with sixty, Incitatus with eighty, Columbus with eighty-eight and Asteropaeus with no less than 107 victories.[64] But these are the exceptions. For the vast majority of gladiators the final curtain fell before they reached thirty.

Grave inscriptions reflect the official differences in status between gladiators. Some inscriptions give only the name of the deceased and the number of fights he had engaged in, others have more to say about his background, his city or country of birth, his family and his status, and whether he was a free man or not. Some gladiators seem to have had wives and even children. One of these was Urbicus. On a marble grave-pillar, probably erected by his wife, we see him with a sword raised in his right hand and a shield in his left. He has removed his helmet with its two eyeholes. The text on his gravestone tells us the following about him:

> This grave is dedicated to the Manes [the souls of men when separated from the body]. For Urbicus, a *secutor* [see page 93]. He belonged to the top category of gladiator (*primus palus*), came from Florence, engaged in thirteen fights and lived for twenty-two years. He is survived by two daughters, Olympia aged five months and Fortunensis, and by his wife, Lauricia, who lived with her respected husband for seven years. I urge you to kill the man who defeated me! His supporters will preserve the memory of Urbicus with honour.[65]

Grave pillar for Urbicus, a *secutor*

It immediately seems odd that in spite of his youth, Urbicus had been married for seven years and had two children. Commentators have suggested that the stonemason made a mistake when chiselling his age, engraving XXII where he meant XXXII. And the anger attributed to Urbicus is quite startling. He calls on people to kill the man who defeated him. He had probably beaten his opponent in an earlier fight but spared his life and now that very same man had killed him. The same bitterness is seen in a Greek inscription from Amisus. The gladiator Diodorus regrets his own benevolence. In his last fight he disarmed his opponent and thought he had won the right to claim victory.[66] But the referee decided otherwise, whereupon the fight resumed and Diodorus was killed after all, going to meet his dark fate.

The few inscriptions that mention marriage have all been found on the grave-pillars of free gladiators. Relationships entered into by slave gladiators were not recognised under Roman law. But these men too would have been eager to explore the possibility of an enduring relationship, regardless of whether or not it would be legally valid. Cohabiting with a woman gave them a sense that their lives were not governed by the gladiator school alone. It is impossible to say how many gladiators lived with women, and in some cases children as well. Probably they formed a small minority. Most gladiators simply did not have the necessary resources. They stayed in the school and had to content themselves with fleeting liaisons.

Their Love Life

Gladiators had plenty of amorous adventures. Women found them extremely sexually attractive, with their

Grave pillar for Diodorus of Amisus, dating from the late second or early third century AD. He is shown victorious, with a sword in each hand

muscular bodies, toned from rigorous training. They were seen as macho, as paragons of masculinity. The word *gladius* (sword) even became a slang term for penis. Many gladiators chose to call themselves something with an erotic flavour like Eros, Hyacinthus or Narcissus, or thought up names that expressed their strength and suppleness: Pugnax (the pugnacious), Ferox (the warlike), Serpentius (the snake) or Tigris (the tiger). Girls scrawled graffiti on the walls of the gladiator schools, declarations of love addressed to particular named gladiators. The graffiti writers did not usually give their own names, but they were probably innocent girls who had visited the arena and fallen in love with a famous gladiator. Sometimes groups of (married) friends got together to write about their hero, a star beyond their reach. When gladiators (or their most fervent supporters) responded to these passionate declarations, they stressed the masculine nature of their feelings. The volcanic ash of Pompeii has preserved a number of these graffiti. Statements such as 'Cresces, with his trident, who catches the girls at night in his net' (*Cresces reti(arius) puparum nocturnarum*), 'Cresces, lord of the girls' (*Cresces puellarum dominus*) and 'Celadus, the Thracian, who makes the girls' hearts beat faster' (*suspirium puellarum tr[aex] Celadus*), show clearly enough the kind of reputation gladiators had.[67] They knew they were popular with women and they would arrange to meet their admirers at some quiet spot near the exercise ground. The infatuation usually wore off on both sides after a while and the gladiator would lose his hold over the girl's heart. But some women could not overcome their obsession with a particular gladiator and wore the evidence of their passionate admiration as they went about their daily lives in the form of hairpins shaped like swords or spears, ideally dipped in the blood of a dead gladiator.

Some felt that the macho behaviour of gladiators was excessive and wrote about it with obvious disdain. One sculptor expressed his abhorrence by making a small statue of a gladiator in the company of the fertility god Priapus. Depictions of this particular god are less than flattering. He is small and malformed with a big, swollen phallus (see p. 72). The artist who created the bronze *tintinnabulum* (literally, small bell) preserved in the Museo Archeologico Nazionale in Naples was even more explicit (see p. 74). It depicts a small male figure, a gladiator, with an enormous sexual organ the nub of which is a head of a dog with lacerating jaws. The dog's head points back up towards the gladiator, threatening him, while the gladiator is about to cut the creature's head off with his dagger. By doing so he will castrate himself. Perhaps his castration is meant to be seen as the ultimate price the gladiator willingly pays for his unbounded lust,[68] but the figurine might equally well represent the view of a bronze caster who was jealous of the gladiator's sex appeal and had thought up this rather gruesome way of poking fun at him.

Only once does a writer explicitly describe a woman who was sincerely in love with a gladiator giving up all she had for her lover. She was the wife of a senator. The author points out that love for gladiators cuts across all social boundaries. The woman in question was called Eppia. She fell in love with a certain Sergius and took refuge with him in Alexandria. Why she fell in love with this particular gladiator is far from easy to explain, since Sergius certainly did not fit the idealised image of a swordsman. This is how

Tufa figurine of a gladiator with Priapus

Juvenal, who recorded the story of this particular pair of lovers, describes him:

> Whose youth and charm have loosed such passion
> in Eppia? For whom does she put up with mockery
> and bear the name of 'gladiatrix'?
> Look, look: it's Sergius. Hardly any beard left
> and declared unfit for combat,
> after one of his arms was severed in a fight.
> And there's a lot else wrong with him besides.
> His skull has been dented by his helmet
> there's a wart on top of his nose
> between two permanently wet, red and swollen eyes.
> But he was once a gladiator, and that confers such
> radiance
> that she does not care at all about fatherland, family,
> hearth and home,
> these are matters of indifference to her; she is in love
> with the iron of his sword, for if this idiot had
> not held a sword, she would never have pleasured him![69]

More tragic than the relationship between Eppia and Sergius was Faustina's impossible love. Faustina was the daughter of Emperor Antoninus Pius (AD 138–161) and the wife of his successor Marcus Aurelius (AD 161–180). The story in the *Historia Augusta* may not be much more than a fantasy, but the mere fact that an empress who had a reputation for seriousness and respectability was said to have fallen in love with a gladiator gives us an idea of how powerfully attractive the gladiators were to women of the upper classes. The story goes that one day Faustina was watching a procession of gladiators go by. She instantly fell in love with one of them. He was on her mind day and

Bronze tintinnabulum showing a gladiator castrating himself

night, but it was impossible for her to get anywhere near him. Her love grew into an obsession and she confessed it to her husband. He consulted the soothsayers, who advised him to kill the gladiator and have Faustina bathe in his blood and then sleep with her husband. And so they did. The gladiator was killed and Faustina's love was extinguished.[70] One rather juicy detail is that she later gave birth to a son, the infamous future emperor, Commodus, who often behaved more like a gladiator than a ruler.

Another empress who seems to have had a relationship with a gladiator is Messalina, the third wife of Emperor Claudius. This is rather less sensational news. Messalina had affairs with many men. She even had a small room in a brothel where she played love games under a pseudonym, Lycisca, literally until she dropped. The exact nature of the relationship is not disclosed in the sources. Cassius Dio tells us only that one of her lovers was Sabinus, a gladiator who was beaten during one of the shows organised by Claudius. Claudius and the spectators wanted him killed, but Messalina made a fervent speech on his behalf and managed to save him from death.[71]

We do not know for certain whether women who fell in love with gladiators ever slept in the barracks with them. There is only one rather tenuous indication. When the ruins of Pompeii were excavated after nearly 1,700 years, in the armoury of the gladiator school, under the many layers of ash, the bodies of seventeen gladiators and a woman were found. She was wearing expensive jewellery: an emerald necklace, two bracelets, rings and a cameo in a small locket. It is hard to say who she was and what she was doing there. Was she the lover of one of them? Was she a prostitute visiting the gladiators, or was she simply a woman caught out by the flow of lava from Vesuvius who fled into the gladiator school armoury for safety?

Female Gladiators

Some women fell under the spell of the gladiator games to such an extent that they decided to step into the arena themselves. Other women were not given a choice but were forced to take up arms. We do not know exactly when women fought for the first time. One organiser of the games in Ostia boasted that he was the first person since the foundation of Rome to put women on the programme,[72] but we cannot determine when he said this. By Nero's time it seems to have become normal practice, since women regularly fought in his shows. They were not always female slaves, foreigners and lower class women, sometimes they were women of the senatorial class. Such fights were probably not a serious part of the programme, to judge by a show put on in Puteoli (Pozzuoli) in AD 63 by Patrobius, a slave freed by Nero, for the visit of the Parthic King Tiridates. In the spirit of his sick-minded emperor he had brought men, women and children from Ethiopia to fight in the arena. How the public responded we do not know. Domitian, an emperor who loved spectacle, had even stranger tastes. He once staged a nocturnal performance in which female gladiators fought either women or dwarves by torchlight – which must surely have been included as a bit of comic relief from the life-and-death games.

Women gladiators most probably did not have to endure the same demanding training as their male colleagues, though they used the same weapons, which Juvenal found very amusing. He believed women ought to stay well away from the arena. Describing their get-up, he can hardly contain his disgust:

Purple dressing gowns and ladies' oil,
who does not know this? But who has never seen a
    woman
behind her defiant shield repeatedly
striking at the exercise pole with her sword
precisely according to the rules of the game?
Such a woman deserves a clarion call – but
just imagine she has more in mind,
that she is training for the real circus.
A helmeted woman like that thinks she can do
    anything,
she is fleeing from her own femininity too, she loves
    power,
although she doesn't want to be a man either: that feels
    too cold!
But if you ever have to sell your wife's
belongings, then you will make a great impression
with a plumed helmet, dagger belt, gauntlets
and a left shin-plate; or if your darling wife
switches to other weaponry and so
throws away her leg protectors you can be proud!
And look, though they are often unable to tolerate
the finest, most expensive robes
and even seem sensitive to silken cloth,
look how they repeat the thrusts they have seen
    demonstrated,
their breath heaving, and look how their little heads
    strain

under such weighty helmets and how
thick bandages of coarse bark support their knees.[73]

Just occasionally, female gladiators inspired real admiration. The two women on a relief from Halicarnassus (first or second century AD), now in the British Museum, are one example. According to the inscription they were called 'Amazone and Achillia', although these were only their stage names. 'Amazone' reminded the audience of the legendary warlike women who fought on horseback and were ruled by a queen, refusing to tolerate the presence of men. 'Achillia' was the female counterpart of Achilles, one of the Greek heroes who had besieged the city of Troy in the mythical past. The

Female gladiators Amazone and Achillia on a relief from
Halicarnassus

women in the relief are equipped in the same way as their male colleagues, except that they are not wearing helmets. The picture probably captures a specific moment. Above the two women is the word *apeluthèsan*, the Greek equivalent of *stantes missae*, which means that the gladiators had fought bravely and were both allowed to withdraw from the arena with honour. But their performance should not be seen as evidence that it was at all common for female gladiators to perform in the arena. The real fans of the gladiator shows were not interested in watching women fight. Emperor Septimius Severus, a military man through and through, believed that these fights were an insult to masculine military virtues and in about AD 200 he banned them. We do not know whether his decision in fact put an end to performances by women in the arena.

What Did It All Cost?

Because gladiator shows attracted such huge crowds at the time of the Roman Empire, the sponsors had to lay down large sums of money to get the most renowned fighters into the arena at all. As long as the state coffers were full and could easily cover the costs, no one really objected. But when the wealth of the empire started to decline, the more sensible emperors started asking themselves whether the sums asked were not in fact quite exorbitant. Emperor Marcus Aurelius, no great fan of the shows, decided in AD 177 that a share of the profits made by gladiator managers and agents should go to the state. Faced with escalating costs as a result of the wars against the Germans in the north, he issued a decree imposing a tax of 25–35 per cent on the agents' earnings.

But the senators persuaded him to withdraw the decree, for they had come up with a more practical proposition. The transcript of the senate debate on the subject has been preserved on a bronze plate in the amphitheatre at Italica, a Roman town near Seville. Although part of the text is missing, we can still follow the argument put by one senator as he addresses the rest. He thanks the emperor for his willingness to withdraw his earlier law and states that the resulting loss to the treasury can be recovered by placing limits on the prices to be charged for gladiators. Future sponsors would not have to come up with so much money to put on a show.

The text mentions five classes of gladiator and four kinds of show, ranging from simple performances to lavish spectacles. No matter what kind of gladiator show it was, an organiser was not allowed to use only gladiators drawn from the five listed classes. Half his gladiators had to be drawn from the lowest category, the so-called *gregarii*, who were to cost between 1,000 and 2,000 *sestertii*. Prices for the top three classes vary between 3,000 and 15,000 *sestertii*. There is a clear relationship between the price charged for a gladiator and the overall cost of putting on a specific show. A sponsor who put on a modest show could sometimes hire a top-class gladiator for less than he would have to pay for a man of even the fourth rank if he were putting on a bigger show, as the following table demonstrates:[74]

price per gladiator (in sestertii)	class of gladiator	cost of show (in sestertii)
3,000	third	30,000–40,000
4,000	second	30,000–40,000

5,000	first	-40,000
5,000	third	40,000-100,000
6,000	second	40,000-100,000
8,000	first	40,000-100,000
5,000	fifth	100,000-150,000
6,000	fourth	100,000-150,000
8,000	third	100,000-150,000
10,000	second	100,000-150,000
12,000	first	100,000-150,000
6,000	fifth	150,000-200,000
7,000	fourth	150,000-200,000
9,000	third	150,000-200,000
12,000	second	150,000-200,000
15,000	first	150,000-200,000

In Rome, gladiator managers rarely if ever dealt directly with the emperor. Instead they negotiated with the *procurator munerum*, the man in charge of organising shows on the emperor's behalf. He was often a freed slave who had worked his way up to a position of trust under the emperor. We no longer know the names of most of these men, although a few have been preserved in inscriptions. The one we know most about, because of an inscription on the sarcophagus containing his remains, is Aurelius Prosenes, who was responsible for running the shows in the Colosseum for many years in the late second century AD:

The freed slaves have had this sarcophagus made at their own expense for their highly esteemed patron Marcus Aurelius Prosenes, freed slave under two emperors, who was allowed access to the emperor's bedchamber. He was responsible for the emperor's possessions and for his treasury; he organised the gladiator shows and was in charge of wine supplies. He was appointed by the now deified Commodus.[75]

There is a second inscription on Prosenes' sarcophagus, which records that he died in May or July AD 217. He was probably freed by Marcus Aurelius, whose son Commodus appointed him organiser of the gladiator shows, a position he held under Septimius Severus and Caracalla as well. The sarcophagus shows that things went well for him financially throughout all those years.

Payments made by the organiser of a show went almost entirely into the pockets of the gladiator managers. The gladiators themselves had to make do with a token payment; only the very top gladiators had a right to a share in the premium. There was no chance of them growing rich on the prize money either. Their reward was usually an olive branch or a wreath, plus a few coins. There were just a few shows in which the prize money was enough to make the winner rich overnight and Tiberius, not exactly a fanatical follower of the gladiator fights, did once hire several famous gladiators who had retired by offering them 100,000 *sestertii* to fight again.[76] Nero even rewarded Spiculus the *murmillo* (see page 89) with a palace[77] and Horace recounts that a gladiator was once allowed to retire to a country villa a wealthy man.[78]

These were the exceptions. For most gladiators the prize money was not enough to pay for a comfortable retirement. There also seems to have been a standard system of percentages worked out between gladiators and agents. Of the already low bonus payments, slave gladiators were allowed to keep only 20 per cent and free

Grave pillar for the *thraex* Satornilus of Smyrna, dating from
the late second or early third century AD

gladiators 25 per cent. The rest went to the *lanista* who
was acting as their agent.[79] With this in mind, it hardly
seems surprising that gladiator managers had such a bad
reputation. Traders were not highly regarded at the best
of times and the fact that a person dealt in human beings
cannot have done much for his reputation. But this would
not have worried a *lanista*. His income was high and the
sponsors could not do without his services. Martial[80]
writes that Hermes, who fought 'with three weapons',
made his boss very rich. Whether Hermes was given any

extra reward as a result is not mentioned, although this does seem quite likely as it would have been in the interests of both men. Seneca believed that every *lanista,* without exception, exploited his gladiators. He compared them to farmers who tend their herds of cows, fattening them up with the ultimate intention of slaughtering them.[81] But Seneca was someone who had little patience with the whole business of gladiator fights. Given the size of the investment they had to make, it is hard to imagine that a gladiator manager would ever deliberately put his best athletes at any greater risk than necessary. Of course he would want to see the highest possible return on his investment, so he could not avoid putting his gladiators up for risky fights. But there was always the reassuring thought that a popular gladiator could rely on clemency from the public as long as he fought courageously, even if he lost.

Only a small number of slave gladiators were able to earn enough money to buy their own freedom, marry, and go on to lead a reasonably comfortable life outside the gladiator school. There must have been many more who signed contracts with the gladiator boss that obliged them to continue appearing in the arena even after they had earned their freedom. It would not have been difficult for the gladiator manager to persuade them to sign, because the opportunities open to former gladiators outside the arena were extremely limited. They were only good at fighting, and yet there was no prospect of a career in the army. So they lived in the hope that a prominent Roman would employ them as part of his team of bodyguards, something that happened fairly regularly in the time of the republic. Later, in the imperial period, former gladiators had to wait and see whether an emperor would decide to engage their services. Only Caligula is known for certain to have recruited gladiators in fairly large numbers and to have appointed several *thraeces* (see page 87) as officers in his German security force. After Caligula's death in AD 41 they were dismissed by Claudius and had to look for another employer. They probably went back into the arena.

Most gladiators in Rome remained in a gladiator school until they died. They sometimes travelled to fights in distant cities, but they were always brought back. They never experienced the pleasures of a carefree life outside the school, supported by their own earnings. The position of veterans of the French Foreign Legion is in some ways similar. They live in a closed community and can never completely break with the profession they entered at a young age, either voluntarily or by force of circumstance. They fight for low pay, most of which they spend on drink and women. Many lose their lives and those who survive face a future of great uncertainty. Once they have served out their contractual term, they try to build a life for themselves outside the barracks, but the rules and norms of civilian life are so utterly unfamiliar that they are often unable to cope and they return to the legion in the sombre knowledge that they will be inextricably bound to it for the rest of their days. Once they have become too physically weak for service, they are housed in special homes where they can look back with nostalgia on their military exploits of times gone by. The fate of most gladiators must have been very similar. If they did not die young they would inevitably reach an age when they had to retire. But since they knew no other world than that of the arena, they remained tied to the gladiator school, the most fortunate among them as trainers or nursing staff, the rest as cleaners or odd job men. Even that kind of work could not last for ever. No longer fit for physical labour, they hung around the barracks telling tales of long ago and begging for alms. Their lives came to an end in the same way as those of most of the Roman proletariat. They died in the street or in hastily constructed turf huts or hovels and their bodies were thrown over the city walls into a deep ravine or buried in mass graves.

Types of Gladiator

A wide range of different kinds of combat was staged for spectators in the Colosseum, none of which had much in common with the early gladiator fights of the third and second centuries BC. In those days the gladiators had been equipped only with spears and lances and fought in a kind of tunic or linen loincloth, holding large circular shields to protect themselves. They did wear bronze helmets. In the course of the first century AD, specific types of combat began to emerge, based on the different weapons involved. Various types of helmet were adopted, the size and shape of the shields changed, the breastplate was introduced and leather straps were wound around the gladiator's right arm. But the most important innovation was that, alongside the lance and the spear, the gladiator was equipped with various kinds of sword and dagger. Opponents now attacked each other with clearly identifiable weapons, which increased the entertainment value as far as the public was concerned, and made the outcome of fights harder to predict.

Although breast armour was available, most gladiators went on fighting bare-chested or in sleeveless tunics.

The heroic nakedness of the upper body made the fights more appealing, but this degree of exposure is remarkable when contrasted with the protection given to the head, legs and sword arm by a heavy helmet, leg-plates and strapping. Perhaps the explanation lies in the origins of the gladiator fight as part of a ceremony at the graveside of a prominent Roman. The gladiators who performed on those occasions were people who had no rights; they were slaves and prisoners, forced to bare their bodies as a sign of subjugation, penance and punishment. This image certainly changed as time went on and gladiators were able to emerge as real heroes, but they must always have been conscious that the emperor and the public had complete power over their lives and that if the decision went against them they would have to offer their necks or backs for the final, fatal thrust, completely naked and powerless.

The earliest gladiators were distinguished by ethnic names: *galli*, *thraeces* and *samnites*, from tribes that had

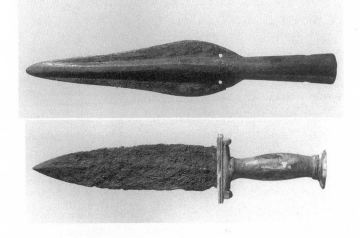

The point of a lance and a short sword

once fought against Rome. The tradition of the *samnites* may go as far back as 308 BC, when the Romans defeated the Samnites, seizing many of their weapons. They gave the weapons to the fighters who were used to add panache to the early funeral games in Rome, so these gladiators became known as *samnites*. In the second century the same happened with Gallic and Thracian weapons. Gradually the fighting methods of these three types of gladiator were adjusted in various ways so that they would have a fair chance against other, later types of gladiator with different equipment.

Most gladiators specialised in a particular set of weaponry throughout their lives. It was rare for any of them to switch weapons. A fighter like Hermes, whom Martial described[82] as good with the lance, the trident and other unspecified weapons, is an exception to the rule. Because of this thoroughgoing specialisation, the fights involved extreme expertise. Organisers could continually pit different categories against each other. Pairs could range from gladiators whose weaponry was (practically) identical to those who had not one single element in common.

We can form a reasonably reliable impression of the various types of gladiator, even though the writers of the ancient world offer only rudimentary technical details. The amazing hoard of ancient paintings, helmets, swords, armour and leg-plates found in Pompeii in 1767 under a thick layer of ash makes up for the lack of written information. Over the past few decades weapons have been found elsewhere too, although on nothing like the same scale. As well as the armaments themselves, we have terracotta statuettes, bronze figures, and pictures of gladiators on headstones,

Helmet found at the gladiator school in Pompeii

mosaics, frescoes and small oil lamps. And then there are the grave inscriptions. The types of gladiator most commonly referred to are *thraeces, murmillones, hoplomachi, retiarii, secutores* (also known as *contraretiarii*), *provocatores, essedarii, dimachaeri, velites, paegniarii, equites* and *andabatae*.

All gladiator shows featured a good number of *thraeces* and *murmillones,* and they often fought each other. A *thraex* was easy to recognise by his relatively small, curved sword (*sica*), much like a dagger, and his small shield (*parma*), which might be either round or square. Since this kind of shield could only be used to cover the chest and stomach, he also wore high leg-plates. The *murmillones* took their name from the *murma,* a salt-water fish that was caught in nets. This was because the *murmillo* was originally mainly put up against the *retiarius* and often got caught in his net. The *murmillo* had a long shield (*scutum*), much bigger than the shield carried by the *thraex,* and he wielded a narrow sword (*gladius*) 40–50 centimetres long. Because his shield was so long, he could make do with short leg-plates that reached no higher than the shin. The *murmillo* also regularly fought the *hoplomachus,* whose equipment looked very similar to the *thraex's*; what distinguished him were a Boeotic helmet and a small round bronze shield. He started fighting with a lance and, if disarmed, would continue with a short sword.

The *retiarius* was a remarkable phenomenon. He looked quite different from all the other gladiators. He had no helmet, no sword and no leg armour, and protective strapping was wrapped around his left rather than his right arm. Across his left shoulder he wore a bronze plate that reached down over his elbow. His body was otherwise unprotected and he wore a small loincloth around his waist. His main weapon was a circular, wide-mesh throwing-net about 3 metres across

Leg-plates found at the gladiator school in Pompeii

and he carried a trident in his other hand. He sometimes used a dagger as well. He could be put up against any of the other types of gladiator, but he was mainly engaged

A *thraex* (right) and a *murmillo* with restored swords

to fight a *secutor*, also known as a *contraretiarius*, a gladiator whose weapons were very like a *murmillo's*. The *secutor's* most obvious distinguishing feature was his helmet, which covered his face and had small holes for the eyes. Since he had a very limited field of vision, he would try to get as close as possible to his opponent, who naturally tried to prevent him. A fight between a *retiarius* and a *secutor* must have been very exciting because the *retiarius*, wildly sweeping his net, demanded the utmost concentration from his opponent if he were to avoid becoming entangled. Once caught in a net, there was no way for a gladiator to escape. On the other hand, once he had missed his chance with the net the *retiarius* became vulnerable and was forced to continue the fight using his trident. The *secutor* now knew he was in with a chance. He parried the trident thrusts with his sword and long shield, looking for an opportunity to disarm his opponent.

The *equites* put on a very different kind of fight. They fought almost exclusively against each other, dressed in loose, multicoloured knee-length tunics. They had medium-sized shields and fought with lances as well as swords. They may well have entered the arena on horseback and only ended up fighting on foot some way into the engagement. We cannot be certain whether this was indeed the type of fight that always marked the start of a gladiator show, as Isidorus of Seville claims.[83]

The *provocatores* mainly fought each other too. They were distinguished by their long, rectangular shields, breastplates, leg-plates on the left leg only, and short swords. The *essedarii* were another of the more striking types. The name is derived from *essedum*, a two-wheeled Celtic war chariot. It must have been quite a spectacular sight when two of these chariots charged towards each other and the combatants engaged at close quarters. We do not know exactly how they fought, nor whether they appeared in all the gladiator games or only the most lavish.

Even less is known about the other types of gladiator. The *dimachaerus* is mentioned twice in inscriptions, but there are no pictorial images of him. To judge by the name, which literally means 'man with two swords', he may have been a gladiator who held a sword or dagger

Fight between a *retiarius* (left) and a *secutor* in a floor mosaic in a villa in Nennig, dating from the first half of the third century AD

in each hand throughout the fight. This would have made it hard for him to defend himself, so this type of fighter could only have been put up against another *dimachaerus*. Even less is known about the *veles*, of whom no images have come down to us. He is believed to have fought armed only with a spear (*iaculum*). The *laquearius* fought with a lasso and seems to have engaged in ferocious combat with the *retiarius,* with his net and trident.

Finally there were gladiators whose fighting techniques were not in the same league as those mentioned above. They were called *paegnarii*. They appeared mainly during the midday break in the programme and amused the audience with tragicomic performances. Without helmets or shields and protected by leather armour, they fought each other. Each man held a whip in one hand and a hooked stick in the other. Fights between *paegnarii* could go on for a long time and would have been looked down on by the 'real' gladiators, because the participants were usually older men with physical disabilities. Even more pathetic were the fights between *andabatae*. Two gladiators, blindfolded or wearing helmets with the eyeholes blocked, attacked one another with swords. This particular act never became especially popular.

The Scene of Action

Shows with large numbers of gladiators produced a thrilling spectacle and attracted vast crowds, so suitable venues were needed. At first open fields with plenty of room for spectators were perfectly adequate. In the second and first centuries BC the scene of the action in Rome was the Roman Forum. A large number of shows were put on here in the open space now bounded on the north side by the Basilica Emilia and the Basilica Porcia and on the south side by the Basilica Sempronia. The spectators sat in the galleries that ran along the sides of the basilicas, on wooden staging that was set up shortly before the performance and was taken down again afterwards. A fire in the Roman Forum in 52 BC cleared the way for improvements. Caesar, by this time living in Gaul, initiated the digging of a long underground passageway beneath the Forum, with steps or ramps in a number of places so that the gladiators could appear suddenly in the arena.

Scribonius Curio is said to have designed and built a revolutionary new amphitheatre that very same year, although this is an unverifiable anecdote noted down by Pliny the Elder, who had doubts himself about how true it was.[84] Apparently Curio had two wooden theatres built, each of which could revolve on an axis. When they were turned towards each other they made an amphitheatre suitable for gladiator fights. Rather less uncertainty surrounds the new theatre that Caesar built on the Campus Martius in 46 BC. It was a *kynegetikon theatron*, a type of theatre originally only used for wild animal chases, but gladiator fights were later held in it as well. Cassius Dio writes that this theatre was called an amphitheatre because there was provision for spectators on every side.[85] It was a wooden building on the south side of the Campus Martius that became redundant when the first stone amphitheatre was built in Rome. Most people knew it as Statilius Taurus' amphitheatre and it was destroyed in the great fire of Rome in AD 64.

In Campania, in the towns of Capua, Liternum and Cumae, special stone amphitheatres were built from the end of the second century BC onwards, their interiors specifically designed for gladiatorial contests. They were elliptical in shape and provided gladiators with enough room to engage in a drawn-out struggle, whether in close combat or while chasing wild animals, an event that had begun to feature more and more often in gladiator

Amphitheatre at Pompeii

shows. There is a marvellous amphitheatre in Pompeii, and better still it can be accurately dated. According to an inscription on the building, it was paid for out of their own pockets by the two highest ranking magistrates in the city, Gaius Quinctius Valgus and Marcus Porcius, and presented to the city in a solemn inauguration ceremony some time not long after 70 BC. It was a large amphitheatre, more than 135 metres long and 104 metres across with an arena of more than 66 by 34 metres. It could accommodate 12,000 spectators. The construction was relatively simple. The lower rows of seating were dug out of the ground, while the upper rows rested on an earthen mound surrounded by a retaining wall. The spectators climbed stairs on the outside of the building to a walkway that ran along the top of the wall with steps leading down to their seats. In the final quarter of the first century BC, a stone amphitheatre was built at Puteoli, with external dimensions of 130 by 95 metres. Paestum followed in the first decades of the first century AD, with an amphitheatre of 100 by 65 metres.

Stone amphitheatres were not built in the Italian provinces alone. All over the Roman Empire, amphitheatres arose that rivalled the facilities in Rome in every respect. The building of an amphitheatre at Lyon (Lugdunum) began in 19 BC and was completed under Tiberius. It demonstrates that Gaul was being romanised very rapidly and that the gladiator games had already become an important entertainment in provincial towns. Representatives of the Gallic people gathered in Lyon once a year to show their loyalty to the Roman emperor by staging games on a grand scale. In subsequent decades amphitheatres were also built in Saintes (Mediolanum Santonum) and Périgueux (Vesunna).

Spain got its first amphitheatre under Augustus, not in one of the romanised coastal towns but in the barren region of Estremadura, deep in the Spanish interior near the border with Portugal. In Mérida, known as Augusta Merita in ancient times, the amphitheatre was built in around 8 BC and its enormous dimensions of 126 by 102 metres and its high raised seating are still impressive. That such a vast amphitheatre should be built here of all places, in a distant corner of the Roman Empire, shows once again how quickly the gladiator shows became popular.

The Building of the Colosseum

Meanwhile, Rome still had to make do with Statilius Taurus' amphitheatre. Nero tried to rectify the situation by giving Rome a new amphitheatre, but it is doubtful whether his wooden structure was more impressive than the facilities in most provincial towns. We shall never know, because this amphitheatre went up in flames when Rome burned in AD 64. But the answer Rome finally produced was stunning. It put all the existing amphitheatres in Italy and more distant provinces firmly in the shade. In AD 70, Emperor Vespasian ordered the building of an amphitheatre that the poet Martial would describe as a new wonder of the world:

Ah, Memphis, speak no more of your marvellous
  pyramids,
    Assyrians, your Babylon turns pale.
The Ionian temple to Diana harvests praise no more,
    the altar of Delos is faded glory now.
The Mausoleum? Ah, it's floating in the air
    but it won't bring the Carians any fame.[86]

All wonders now make way for Caesar's work!
People talk of just one thing and nothing else.[87]

The official name was *Amphitheatrum Flavium*, but since the Middle Ages it has been known as the Colosseum, a reference to the great bronze statue of Nero, the *Colossus Neronis*, that once stood not far away in the hallway of Nero's monumental palace, the *Domus Aurea*. This golden palace had become a symbol of Nero's arrogance and extravagance and it aroused widespread resentment among the population. A lake in the grounds of the palace, between the Velian, Esquilline and Caelian Hills, was chosen as the site of the Colosseum. The location had been carefully selected not only for the favourable terrain, but also with the notion that it might be possible to bring a dignified end to what had been a less than happy period for Rome. Nero had ruled Rome as a tyrant and the civil wars of AD 68-69 that followed his death had created deep divisions in society. The Colosseum was to be a symbol of a new era in which the emperor and his people would be bound together in a way that afforded dignity to both sides. Unpleasant memories could then be set aside for good.

Vespasian's architects succeeded in draining the lake and keeping it dry using drainage canals. Tens of thousands of people must have worked on the scheme. Rumour had it that as well as slaves and citizens, who were happy to earn a little money for their labour, more than 10,000 Jewish prisoners of war who had been deported to Rome after the destruction of Jerusalem in AD 70 were put to work on this monumental building project. Martial says of the end result of Vespasian's efforts:

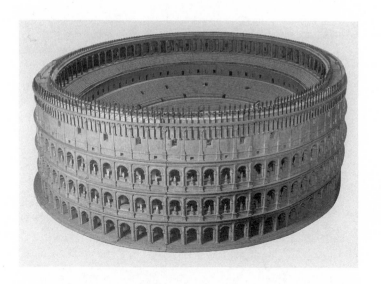

Model of the Colosseum by Carlo Lucangeli and Paolo
Dalbono, 1824

On this spot, where now Colossus towers up
> towards the stars and podiums rise in the streets,
the loathed imperial palace once stood proud,
> one single house taking possession of the entire
> city.
Now a vast and marvellous arena stands
> where Nero's squelching morass used to lie.
Where we now see hot baths, built at great speed,
> there once lay a park that made poor wretches
> homeless.
Where now the Claudian portico throws its shadow,
> the royal domain once had its outer limits.
Rome has regained itself! Thanks to Caesar's goodwill
> the people take their pleasure where once the
> tyrant did.[88]

A passageway under the Colosseum where the lifts were
installed to hoist animals up to the arena

It took ten years to build and every inhabitant of Rome must have watched its progress with growing astonishment and admiration. First the drained lake was dug out and more than 30,000 tons of earth removed. Then foundations of concrete and solid rock were laid, 3–4 metres deep under the arena, and 8–12 metres deep under the load-bearing columns, which were made of a rock called travertine. The whole amphitheatre was constructed on the principle that the seven concentric rings of columns should be able to bear the total weight. The seating is supported by the columns of the internal walls. These are staggered back slightly so that they can directly support the arched constructions under the seats. Enormous amounts of travertine – estimates suggest more than 100,000 tons – were brought from the mines at Tivoli in the Alban Hills not far from Rome along a specially laid road. The slabs of marble that would decorate the walls and line the senators' thrones were brought from far and wide, as was the iron used to clamp the blocks of travertine together. Shape and dimensions were carefully calculated. The structure can be seen as having one axis 188 metres long and another of 156, with a circumference of 527 metres. The arena measures more than 80 x 45 metres with a surface area of over 3,600 square metres. The arena is separated from the tiers of seating by a wall almost 4 metres high, with entrances for the gladiators at the far ends and access on either side for the emperor, his entourage and the Vestal Virgins.

The sturdy floor of the arena was covered with a deep layer of sand. We do not know what the space under the floor looked like when the Colosseum was inaugurated in AD 80 under Emperor Titus, because the complex arrangement of gangways and small rooms, the ruins of which are still clearly visible today, was laid out by Titus' brother Domitian who succeeded him in AD 81. His architects divided the space below the arena, the *hypogeum*, into four sections by creating two absolutely straight passageways perpendicular to each other along the two central axes of the building. Down here under the ground within the outer wall stood the cages where the wild animals waited for a day or two prior to the show for their one and only performance in the arena. Several hours before the performance started, the gates of the cages were raised and the animals were driven through a narrow passageway no more than 55 centimetres wide. They could only move in one direction, towards the waiting lifts. When the signal came for the animals to enter the arena, the cage hoists ⁓ were raised to the next level with the help of counter-weights. The animals were then driven out of the lift cages and forced along gently sloping ramps and steps through the open trap doors into the arena. All kinds of material needed for the lunchtime executions or appropriate pieces of scenery could be lifted up very quickly this way as well. The arena could be transformed into a forested stage set in just a few minutes.[89]

The outer walls are almost 52 metres high, and consist of four levels: on the ground floor are eighty arches with engaged Doric columns, and on the first and second floors the same number of arcades enclosed by Ionic and Corinthian columns; the top floor has no arches framed by pillars but rather a solid wall with square Corinthian columns embedded in it and rectangular windows. Building work was completed in AD 80, but Titus' brother Domitian later enlarged the Colosseum by adding a top ring of seating on the fourth floor. This was made of wood and crowned with a colonnade of eighty marble pillars.

When the galleries were designed, the needs of the spectators were paramount. Everyone was to have a good view of the entire fight scene no matter where they were sitting. It was equally important that they could find their seats quickly. The seating was divided into three zones (*caveae*), each consisting of sixteen wedge-shaped sections (*cunei*). Every ticket showed in exactly which section, row and seat someone was sitting, for example *Cun V, In(feriori) (gradu decimo) VIII* (in section 5, on the lower row 10, seat number 8). Standing in the public square that surrounded the Colosseum, the spectators could clearly see which door they needed to go through from the numbers over the seventy-six public entrances. Each entrance led to a circular corridor (*ambulacrum*) with doorways under the seating that gave on to a passageway from which the visitors could reach their places via steps and entryways (*vomitoria*). Signs pointed the way. The higher the seat, the more spacious the concentric corridor below it and the longer the flights of steps.

People from different walks of life did not sit next to each other. Within the Colosseum, the divisions between the various groups that made up Roman society were maintained in every respect. In the lowest row of seats, on a raised platform (*podium*) 4 metres above the arena, sat the most prominent Romans, often dressed in white togas. The emperor had the best seat of all in a kind of box (*pulvinar*) in the first row at the centre of one of the longer sides of the arena. He could go straight to his box through his own private entrance and leave before the show finished if necessary. It was not unusual for him to be joined there by male family members or important guests, who could sit in comfortable chairs to watch the games. Directly opposite him on the other side, the organiser of the games sat in his own box (*tribunal editoris*) along with the empress, magistrates and Vestal Virgins. The remaining seats in the bottom row were reserved for the senators, some of whom must have been regular visitors who always sat in the same places, since their names have been carved into the seats.

In the next few rows up, known as the 'lower tribunes' (*ima cavea*), seats were reserved for the knights and the *decuriones*, the governors of provincial towns. The less important a person was, the higher up he sat. The rows immediately above them, the 'middle tribunes' (*media cavea*) were occupied by wealthy Roman citizens, often wearing special multicoloured togas. Above them began the *summa cavea*, the 'highest tribunes' where the poor citizens sat alongside freed slaves and foreigners. Above them again, at the very top of the amphitheatre (*summum maenianum in ligneis*), sat the wives and daughters of senators, knights and prosperous citizens, protected by a high parapet from the gaze of inquisitive spectators below. It is possible that the hierarchy was maintained even on the women's tribune so that the wives and daughters of senators sat further forward. It is certainly remarkable that such an enormous distinction was made between the Vestal Virgins, who were allowed to watch the gladiator fights from the front row, and the rest of the socially prominent women who were banished to just below the roof. Perhaps this had to do with the gladiators' reputation for breaking hearts. The emperors may have wanted to prevent senators' wives from having eye contact with their heroes in the arena. Women who, like Eppia and Messalina, gave in to the temptation of an amorous adventure with a gladiator were generally ostracised. People were less worried by the prospect when it came to the Vestal Virgins. As priestesses of the goddess Vesta they were fulfilling an official function closely related to that of the emperor in his role as *pontifex maximus* (high priest of the Roman state religion). The reasoning behind their seating arrangements was probably that these chosen women knew perfectly well that eternal chastity was required of them and that if they ever went against this command they would be punished in the worst way imaginable, by being buried alive.

There were always many people with non-Italian backgrounds among the ordinary visitors, because by the end of the second century BC Rome had become an extremely attractive place for anyone from the provinces. From the late republic onwards, thousands came to Rome from far and wide, settling in the city and making a living for themselves as tradesmen or artisans. They quickly became integrated into Roman society and were just as likely to be regular spectators of the gladiator shows as the native Romans. According to Martial, many members of foreign tribes were present at the opening of the Colosseum:

What nation is so far away, which place has
    remained so backward
that its people do not want to come and look at
    Caesar's city?
The rough Thracian mountain people come, the
    Sarmatans come

Their lips still wet with horses' blood,
and people from the sources of the Nile
or coasts on the very edges of the world.
Arabs hasten here, Sabaians hasten here,
Cilicians in clouds of native
perfume, Germans with their hair sticking up
and Negroes with their short and curly hair.
You can hear every language in this place. But they
   all say the same thing:
'Oh Caesar, true father of the State!'[90]

Martial is talking about foreigners who had settled
permanently in Rome. But there were also people from
the provinces who would make a special trip to Rome
for the gladiator fights and go home again after a 'week
at the Colosseum'. Some travelled a long way to get
there, from the east or from the far west. One man from
Baetica in south-eastern Spain took more than a month
to reach Rome, but the journey back home took far
longer still. He was blown off course in a storm and only
reached home months later, after a period of
considerable hardship. A small number of spectators
from distant lands came back fairly regularly, but these
were very well-to-do people with their own seats in the
Colosseum, which they rented for an extended period
so that they would always be assured of a good position.

Safety

Part of the popularity of the gladiator shows arose from
the fact that the city authorities made sure that the
safety of the audience was reasonably well catered for.
The surviving remains of amphitheatres in the Roman

Empire show that the architects took their work extremely seriously. Nevertheless, there was always the chance of a collapse due to faulty construction, earthquakes or fire. As far as we can tell, the Colosseum was spared any catastrophic disasters during the first three centuries of its existence. But it was affected by earthquakes and fire on several occasions and performances had to be cancelled for a period. Extensive renovations were carried out under Emperor Antoninus Pius, but they were nowhere near as thorough as the repairs that were done under Heliogabalus and Alexander Severus. On 23 August AD 217, during Macrinus' short-lived regime, lightning struck the wooden passageway that ran around the top of the building and flames swept through the wooden seating and damaged the stone tribunes below. The fire even spread to the cramped holding bays and cells beneath the arena, causing extensive damage. The stone had become porous and when the waterspouts were turned on, parts of the outer wall and stone seating collapsed. It was impossible to hold any shows in the Colosseum for a period of almost six years and it only re-opened in AD 223, amid great celebrations. As far as we know, this was the biggest fire to hit the Colosseum before the end of the gladiator shows in the fifth century.

The greatest danger the spectators faced came from the arena itself. No one could ever be completely confident that a vindictive gladiator facing imminent defeat would not sling his weapon into the crowd out of sheer despair. It was also impossible to predict how the wild animals might react when men with flaming torches chased them out of their cages into the arena. When leopards, tigers and lions (to name only the most dangerous of the animals) were suddenly driven out from the darkness of their underground confinement into full daylight, to a deafening roar from the gallery, they must have been crazed with terror. The keepers kept the animals hungry prior to the performance so that they would leap after their prey immediately on entering the arena. But in their panic the animals sometimes reacted unexpectedly and turned their pent-up aggression and frustration on the very people who had come to be entertained.

The most eye-catching of the potential targets were the emperor and senators in the front row, divided from the arena by a wall about 4 metres high – not high enough for the honoured guests to feel completely safe should an angry tiger pounce, since tigers are capable of leaping higher than 4 metres. Rollers were placed on top of the wall as an elementary safety precaution, to prevent a wild animal from getting a foothold, but because the emperor and senators did not regard this as enough to allow them to relax as they watched the animals being taunted, a temporary wooden barrier was erected several metres from them in the arena. It had iron hooks or elephant tusks on top of it with a net fixed to them, which fell down in folds to the arena floor several metres away where it was attached to stone pedestals. Should an animal succeed in jumping over this protective barrier, it would end up on the path between the 4-metre wall and the temporary partition, where security staff could immediately rush over and tackle it. The partition was removed as soon as the animal fights were over.

The organisers must also have needed to take the possibility of rioting into account. After all, a day at the Colosseum was a day of brutal violence. The spirit of the arena must sometimes have inflamed passions in the galleries above. For the Roman plebs, the Colosseum and the Circus Maximus were the only places where they could let rip their emotions, their aggression and pent-up frustration, in front of the emperor and senators. An unpopular emperor whose show had disappointed the spectators or one who had failed politically, by being unable to provide sufficient grain for example, would receive an unambiguous message. The crowd might start jeering and throwing anything they could lay their hands on. But far more often, supporters of different sides would have set on each other. For each fight they were divided into two camps. Their choice was guided less by sympathy for one or other of the gladiators than by the gladiator's weapons and method of fighting. On one side were the *parmularii*, fans of the fighters who used a small round shield (*parma*), the most important of which were the *thraeces*. Against them were the *scutarii*, supporters of the fighters who used a large elongated shield (*scutum*), such as the *murmillones* and the *secutores*. There must have been many occasions when the 'winning side' hurled insults at the losers, who refused to take this abuse lying down and laid into the other side with their fists with inevitable consequences. Probably such riots were limited in scale and fairly easily quelled. As I mentioned, different social groups were strictly separated, so traditional conflicts between classes could not easily be fought out in the amphitheatre. All the same, it is possible that spectators in a given section would occasionally climb the dividing wall *en masse* to attack another section. Faced by this kind of situation the authorities had the option of calling on the 7,000 strong praetorian guard, charged with

The riots in Pompeii, depicted in a mural dating from the
second half of the first century AD

ensuring the safety of the emperor and his family, and the
special city cohorts of more than 3,000 men. This
amounted to a police force deemed capable of suppress-
ing any disturbances in or near the Colosseum. The fact
that ancient sources are silent on the subject of public
disorder seems to point to good crowd control. On the

other hand if we look at the riots that took place in AD 59 in the amphitheatre at Pompeii, it seems almost certain that in Rome too, the situation before, during and after the performances must sometimes have been explosive. The riots in Pompeii broke out during a gladiator show organised by a certain Livineius Regulus, a man with a dubious reputation. The exact circumstances are unclear, but according to Tacitus,[91] who reports on these events in his own typically terse and detached manner, groups of supporters from Pompeii and nearby Nuceria attacked each other. It began relatively innocently, with cursing on both sides. Then they started stoning each other and finally grabbed weapons. The supporters from Pompeii were in the majority and got the upper hand in the battle that ensued. Most of the victims were Nucerians. An unknown number died and others had such severe stab wounds that their arms or legs had to be amputated. After a judicial inquiry, the people of Pompeii were banned from organising gladiator shows for ten years.

Comfort

Because gladiator shows lasted a full day, from early morning until evening, the organisers were well advised to ensure that visitors were comfortable. An agreeable place to sit was the primary requirement, but this was often impossible to find, especially in the higher sections where the seats were closer together than in the lower rows. The hard stone seating was not exactly conducive to a lengthy sit, but most spectators got around this by bringing cushions with them.

Far more of a problem was the summer heat. On windless days, when the temperature in the amphitheatre could easily rise above 30 degrees C at midday, conditions in the galleries were unpleasant and everyone longed for shade and a way to cool down. Perhaps this is one of the reasons why Augustus decided to schedule gladiator shows in the cooler months of March and December. But an emperor could always find a reason to hold games in the summer as well: a victory on the borders of the empire, a birthday, the commemoration of an imperial jubilee. Large awnings were used to protect the spectators from unbearably high temperatures.

Research suggests that 240 iron masts were erected around the Colosseum, set in large plinths with vertical oblong holes (a few of which can still be seen on the north and east sides). On top of the masts were wooden beams which formed a kind of suspension bridge system. With the aid of hoists and pulleys, the beams, resting on consoles at the rim of the amphitheatre, were lowered so that sails strung on cables could be stretched out over the galleries. Remnants of this system are still visible in the form of large pulleys, rather like mooring capstans, used to tauten the ropes attached to the sails. A special unit of the fleet from Misenus (in the Bay of Naples), based near the Colosseum, was charged with the task of manning the installation. Neither the arena nor the podium for members of the elite was covered; the emperor and his entourage sat under parasols and umbrellas.

Because it could become oppressively hot in spite of the awnings, and because the stink of blood and human sweat hung heavy on the air, a special sprayer system was used to squirt the crowds with a mixture of water and saffron, wine, or balsam. The water was probably pumped up from large tanks through pipes to spraying devices high on the upper edge of the amphitheatre, concealed behind attractive statues. Not everyone was happy with this cooling mechanism, especially if the nozzles had not been adjusted properly and the spectators got squirted with thick jets of water.

Many visitors took a short break at lunchtime to go and get something to eat nearby. The most affluent among them visited local bars where light meals were served and, more importantly, wine. Others bought light snacks and cups of wine at little stalls around the Colosseum. The rest of the crowd brought their own food and drink with them and stayed in their seats all day, afraid of losing their places or missing the public executions that took place around midday. But for them too, the moment inevitably came when they had to leave their seats for a call of nature. Most amphitheatres – and in this the Colosseum was no exception – had only rudimentary toilet facilities, a form of urinal for both men and women, in which they could urinate but nothing else. For proper toilets they had to leave the Colosseum and make use of public conveniences, which were areas screened off by three partitions in a horse-shoe shape concealing a large number of toilets. People would sit on a marble rim around a large hole with a slot at the front to facilitate cleaning. Beneath the bench ran a sewer trench with water continually flowing through it to flush away the excreta. The water ran into the public sewer. By Roman standards these toilets were reasonably clean, but so many people used them during the midday break that they must quickly have become a filthy mess. Ancient authors do not make any mention of the state of hygiene up in the galleries, but by evening the Colosseum must have looked very dirty indeed, with rubbish and leftover food lying everywhere.

Copies of the Colosseum

Even before the Colosseum was officially opened, word spread across the empire that an amphitheatre of unprecedented beauty was being built in Rome. It became a landmark, part of the sightseeing tour even when no festivities were taking place. Architects admired the solid construction, asked for architectural drawings, and made plans for amphitheatres modelled after the Colosseum to be built in provincial towns. It was not admiration for the architectural beauty of the Colosseum alone that inspired local authorities to start building their own; they were also keen to demonstrate their solidarity with the client Emperor Vespasian. He had restored the unity of the empire and created the necessary conditions for the economy to flourish once more. What better way to organise an emperor cult than by building an amphitheatre modelled on the Colosseum?

One of the first towns in Italy to start building a Colosseum-style amphitheatre was Puteoli, a rich port city (Pozzuoli, near Naples). Inscriptions show that the main financial backers were trade organisations established by rich merchants. And the results were far from disappointing: an amphitheatre built on flat land just outside the city, measuring 149 by 116 metres on the outside, with an exterior wall three storeys high, that could accommodate more than 28,000 spectators. In contrast to the outer walls, of which only scattered chunks of marble remain, the 75 by 42 metre arena is still intact. The underground passageways, animal pens and cells are all clearly visible, as are the steps the gladiators would have climbed up to enter the arena and the places where the hoisting mechanisms were installed for lifting the wild animals. There were awnings here too.

In northern Italy, Verona had an impressive amphitheatre.[92] Again the dimensions are considerable: 152 by 103 metres with an outer wall made up of arcades on three levels. Four concentric rings of walls supported the seating, reached by the 25,000 visitors via seventy-two entrances and sixty-four flights of steps.

In the south of France, which was part of the province of Gallia Narbonensis in ancient times, two almost identical amphitheatres arose in the towns of Arles (Arelate) and Nîmes (Nemausus), both designed by the same architect. In Arles part of the existing city had to be demolished to build the amphitheatre, which had room for 23,000 people. With a maximum length of 136 metres, a maximum width of 107 metres and an arena

A seventeenth-century engraving showing the amphitheatre in Arles

measuring 69 by 38 metres, it is still the most eye-catching monument in modern Arles, which has grown up around the amphitheatre. Here too, the social hierarchy was reflected in the seating arrangements. In the lowest rows sat the town officials and the often very wealthy members of the most important trade organisations, while the poorer citizens, freed men and slaves sat further up. The amphitheatre in Nîmes is slightly smaller, 132 by 101 metres, but in all other respects it is clearly inspired by the venue at Arles and even better preserved. Its attractive colonnades, the arches in the façade and the system of stairways illustrate how important the gladiator shows had become in Gaul by the late first century.

By the third century AD there were over 200 amphitheatres across the Roman empire. In fact it seems that affection for the emperor and the popularity of the gladiator shows led to an unprecedented building boom in the first and second centuries AD. The majority of amphitheatres were small, with space for an audience of a few thousand people, but some were very large, such as the one built in the late first century AD in the port city of Pola, Colonia Pietas Julia (Pula, in Istria). The external walls, with double arcades built into them, have a maximum length and breadth of 132 by 105 metres. It was obviously constructed in the same tradition as the amphitheatres at Arles and Nîmes. Perhaps the most picturesque amphitheatre of all is the one at El Djem (Thysdrus) in Tunisia. Attractively situated at the edge of the modern city, its dimensions are impressive at 149 by 124 metres. It had space for nearly 40,000 spectators. Remarkably, it was built in the third century, around AD 230, when Gordianus I, very briefly emperor in AD 235,

Amphitheatre at El Djem

was governor of the province of Africa Proconsularis. It would seem things were not going so badly in North Africa as they were in the rest of the empire, since it is otherwise hard to explain how the city could have raised enough money to pay for such a monumental structure.

Most amphitheatres are found in areas that once belonged to the western part of the Roman empire (see the list at the end of this book). There are far fewer in the east and in general most of them are small. This might indicate that the Greek-speaking population was less interested in the bloodthirsty gladiator shows. On the other hand, a lot of gladiator inscriptions have been found in the east. The most likely explanation probably lies in the building methods. The arenas of most amphitheatres in the eastern provinces were dug out of the ground, so fewer traces of them remain. Also, towns such as Perge, Cyzicum and Ephesus already had good theatres, which could have been converted into suitable venues for gladiator shows by carrying out minor alterations such as erecting an additional wall or an extra set of railings to protect spectators sitting in the bottom rows.

Some cities in the western provinces did not have the resources to build both a theatre and an amphitheatre, so they made the best of things by building combined venues where stage plays as well as gladiator fights could be held, a hybrid theatre-cum-amphitheatre design. While the gladiator fights were going on, the lowest row of seats was left empty. There was a good example of this kind of semi-amphitheatre at Lutetia (Paris). An elliptical arena was surrounded by tiers of seating like a real amphitheatre, but on the western side a gap in the seats was taken up by a huge stage. While gladiator fights were being held, the stage was screened off behind a high partition.

The Animals

From the moment the Romans first discovered exotic animals in their colonies, they set about establishing an almost constant supply. As early as the third century BC, they introduced elephants into their victory parades, and these elephants made such an impression that they started a trend. Time and again, some astonishing new member of the animal kingdom would be presented to the public, first in parades and victory processions. A hundred years later they were being used in hunting events and animal fights as well. Like the gladiator fights, these events grew rapidly in scale. In 104 BC, after the Romans had defeated Iugurtha, king of Numidia, an ancient region in North West Africa, the *aediles* Licinius Crassus and Mucius Scaevola organised a hunting show in the Circus Maximus with 100 lions.[93] In 99 BC the first show to feature elephants fighting each other was put on by Claudius Pulcher.[94] A little over forty years later, Marcus Scaurus presented the crowd with 150 leopards, a hippopotamus and five crocodiles.[95] Three years after that, Pompey took things to another level again. He held games in which twenty elephants, 600 lions, 410 leopards and innumerable apes were killed. As special attractions he introduced a Northern European lynx and a rhinoceros.[96] This must have been one of the largest hunting shows in Roman history, prior to the opening of the Colosseum. Even Caesar was unable to trump his great rival. In 46 BC, shortly after he became dictator for life, he put a very large number of elephants on display, along with 400 lions, several bulls from Thessaly (now Macedonia) and a giraffe.[97] Not even Augustus, who prided himself on the fact that a total of 3,500 wild animals had been killed in his shows including many lions, leopards, bears and even crocodiles, could match the large numbers in single events that Pompey managed to produce. In 2 BC 260 lions and thirty-six crocodiles were slaughtered in honour of his grandsons and a further 200 lions were killed in AD 12.[98] Caligula put 400 bears and 400 unnamed African wild animals into one of his shows and Nero once had 400 bears and 300 lions killed in a single day.[99] At the inauguration of the Colosseum, 9,000 animals were killed in games that went on for several weeks.[100] Trajan beat this record by a good margin, with 11,000 animals killed.[101] The emperors who succeeded Trajan were aware that it was no longer just a matter of the number of wild animals killed, but how many different kinds and how exotic or unusual they were. In the show Antoninus Pius put on in AD 149 there were elephants, hyenas, lions, tigers, rhinoceroses, crocodiles and hippopotamuses.[102]

By the third century AD, economic recession made it increasingly difficult to stage events with an appropriate number of spectacular-looking wild beasts. *Historia Augusta* – which gives us the biographies of the third-century emperors – suggests that the supply of wild animals was still perfectly adequate. Emperors continued to put on large-scale, costly games with thousands of beasts. But a closer look reveals a crucial difference. There has clearly been a shift from the meat-eating predators to herbivores. Long before the highest honours were

Mosaic showing wild animals, dating from the third century AD

conferred upon Gordianus I in AD 235, he had already staged twelve shows with wild animals. During one of these games he staged a mass hunt with 200 deer, 30 wild horses, 100 wild sheep, 10 elk, 100 bulls, 300 ostriches, 30 wild donkeys, 150 bears, 200 chamois and 200 red deer.[103] There is no mention of lions, tigers or leopards. His grandson Gordianus III (AD 238–244) did not want to be outdone. To celebrate his victory against the Persians he had 32 elephants, 10 elk, 10 tigers, 60 tame lions, 30 tame leopards, 10 hyenas, 6 hippopotamuses, 1 rhinoceros, 10 bears, 10 giraffes, 20 wild donkeys, 40 wild horses and a large number of other wild animals brought to Rome.[104] Predators certainly feature in this list, but a large number of them are tame. In any case, Gordianus III never got a chance to put on his show: he was killed before it could take place.

By this point the trend was probably to use mainly grazing animals. During the several days of games organised by Emperor Probus in AD 281, the arena of the Circus Maximus was transformed into a forest for a day and 1,000 ostriches, 1,000 deer, 100 wild boar, gazelles, ibex and innumerable other herbivores appeared among the trees. There were no lions this time, although they did feature on the programme for one of the subsequent days. The 100 lions brought out to fight, however, turned out to be tame. To the disappointment of both the organisers and the public, there was no sense of spectacle as they were killed.[105]

It was changes in the environments where African and Asian predators lived that caused the shows to be adjusted. More and more natural landscapes in North Africa had been turned into grain fields, olive orchards and vineyards, which inevitably drove the animals further south. In areas where predators had managed to survive, uncontrolled hunting meant that their numbers declined until they gradually disappeared altogether. It seems beyond doubt that the slaughter in the amphitheatres had disastrous consequences for animal populations. The killing of thousands of animals in every show over several centuries must have driven certain species to complete extinction in some regions. We have firm evidence that the lion died out in Libya as a result of the hunts. The Libyans were delighted by this, as is clear from the following lines of a poem in the *Anthologia Palatina*, in which an emperor is praised for removing the fear of attack by lions:

> Borders of the Libyan Nasamonians
> No longer are your plains inaccessible
> Because of all those wild beasts.
> No longer do you hear the echo
> Of lions roaring in the desert.
> The young emperor has captured the entire pride
> And set them up against his fighters.
> The mountains, once home to wild beasts,
> Have been transformed into pastureland.[106]

At first all this had little effect on the supply of wild animals. The emperors simply concluded that if animals could no longer be found 'close to home' they would have to be brought from further afield. So hunters penetrated deeper and deeper into unknown territories, as far as India and Ethiopia. By the third century AD however, a combination of scarcity, increasing costs of transport and lack of money meant that demand could no longer be met. Organisers of shows were forced to make changes to the programme.

We know nothing about the costs of all those

thousands of animals brought to Rome every year for the first two centuries of the imperial era. None of the sources mention anything about payments to hunters or to those in charge of transport. The veil is lifted slightly by the 'Magerius Mosaic', which dates from the beginning of the third century AD. It was found in a house not far from El Djem in Tunisia. The floor mosaic shows fighting scenes: four huntsmen, all members of the hunting association (*sodalitas venatorum*) of the Telegenii, face four leopards, each with its own name. The organiser of the show, Magerius, is also depicted in the mosaic. Next to him are the words:

Announcement from the herald.
Sirs, in order that the Telegenii may be
in receipt of your sympathy in return for a leopard,
give them 500 denarii [2,000 sestertii].

The 'Magerius Mosaic'

So they must have agreed that 500 *denarii* would be paid to each of the four huntsmen who had caught the leopards, that is, the men depicted fighting them. But at the centre of the mosaic a man is shown holding a tray with four small bags on it. Rather than the agreed 500 *denarii* per man, the bags contain 1,000 for each of them. The following words appear next to this image:

> Applause. May future sponsors of the gladiator games learn from your example. May an echo as great as the payments you have made reach earlier sponsors. Who has ever put on a show and when? You will put on a gladiator show at your own expense, one that equals the standard of the shows of the *quaestor*. This will be your day! This is what it means to be rich and powerful. This is it! Night has fallen. May the Telegenii leave your show with their bags of money.[107]

The show must have been such a great success that Magerius was happy to pay the Telegenii double the price, eager to be seen as a true benefactor in his native city.

The amount laid down by Magerius was insignificant compared to the prices the organisers had to pay for hunting shows later in the third century. In AD 301, Emperor Diocletian issued a Price Edict in which he fixed prices for the transport and sale of all sorts of goods. Steadily increasing inflation had clearly driven prices up so much over the previous decade that the government had been forced to intervene. Diocletian set the prices of around 1,000 items and it became an offence to charge more. Several species of wild animal were on the list and all of them had become particularly expensive because they were so scarce. We read in the edict that the cost of a lion could be between 125,000 and 150,000 *denarii*, a lioness now cost between 100,000 and 125,000 *denarii*, a leopard cost 70,000 *denarii*, and the maximum amount asked for a bear had risen to between 20,000 and 25,000 *denarii*. Herbivores were much cheaper. An ostrich cost 5,000 *denarii*, a wild boar 4,000–6,000, a deer 2,000–3,000 and a wild donkey a maximum of 5,000 *denarii*.[108]

Capturing and transporting all these wild animals required a huge number of people. The first job for the organiser or his official representative was to estimate how many animals were needed for a show that might last several days or a week. His estimate took into account the large number of animals that would die during transport. He then got in touch with the provincial governors. The governors acted as inter-mediaries and they and their staff investigated whether or not the supply of game in the areas under their jurisdiction was sufficient to meet requirements. They then dispatched parties of local huntsmen or army units specially trained to catch wild animals. Inscriptions have been found in Germany and Switzerland in which soldiers are referred to as *ursarii* (bear hunters). In one inscription a centurion boasts that he has caught fifty bears in six months. Some soldiers were given the job of looking after the animals in special *vivaria* (fenced areas with stables, rather like zoos) until it was time to transport them to Rome or elsewhere.[109]

The huntsmen never operated alone but always in groups composed of members of the associations they had set up. We know about a few of these associations from inscriptions: the Telegenii have already been mentioned, the names Pentasii and Taurisci also appear.

Once they had determined where the lions, tigers, bears or elephants lived, the huntsmen would spread out across the animals' territory and dig traps in various places. They were simple but effective. In the middle of a pit they made a pillar out of earth, stone or wood and then tied a lamb or a goat to the top of it in such a way that the animal would cry out desperately with pain. The edges of the pit were raised with mounds of earth or wooden fencing, so the predator would leap at its prey without being able to tell that there was an empty space beneath it. It would run up, jump over the edge, fall into the pit and discover that it could not climb out. The huntsmen then lowered a cage with a piece of meat in it as bait. The moment the desperate animal entered the cage a gate was lowered and the animal was trapped.

Armed horsemen with burning torches would often chase elephants into a valley between two steep hills. When the elephants had no escape routes left, the hunters would close off the valley with nets and wait until the animals were so exhausted that they could get close enough to tie their feet together. Sometimes this kind of hunt failed because just as they were about to be captured, the animals were helped out of their predicament by other elephants. A group would stand on the hilltop above and disturb the ground so much that there would be a landslide, giving the trapped animals a chance to escape. Nets were also used to catch tigers, leopards, lions and other predatory animals. Hunters on horseback, well protected by their shields and holding burning torches, chased the animals into an enclosed space where nets were thrown over them. Sometimes this enclosed space led to a narrow shaft, which had a wide cart with a cage on it positioned at the far end. The animals could move in only one direction. When the gate dropped their days of freedom were over.

Now came the most difficult part of the whole operation, the transporting of the animals. In their cages they were placed on heavy carts and taken to a holding area and then on to the nearest sea port, where they were handed over to the dealers who had signed a contract with the Colosseum authorities agreeing to transport the animals and their keepers. The vast majority of animal traders were members of an association (*collegium*). Some of these corporations or private companies traded in all species of animals and had representatives in cities right across the Roman Empire. Others specialised in particular animals, such as elephants or lions. Because of the costly purchase and transport agreements and the huge financial risks involved, only a few dealers were truly independent. Sometimes the task of transporting the animals was entrusted to the staff of the *cursus clabularis*, the imperial heavy goods transport service, which operated in close consultation with the staff of the Colosseum.

The animals travelled across the Mediterranean Sea on specially equipped cargo ships. These were probably ships with converted cargo holds and upper decks fitted out to take cages. The remainder of the hold was used to carry food for the animals: plenty of small livestock for the predators and tons of hay or straw for the large herbivores and grazing animals. These ships would be large galleys rather than real sailing ships. Galleys offered less cargo space, on the other hand the fact they could be rowed meant they were less dependent on the weather and therefore more reliable, especially if the

Embarkation of the animals depicted in the large hunting mosaic in the Piazza Armerina, dating from the fourth century AD

wind was blowing in the wrong direction. The ship in the large mosaic in the Piazza Armerina in Sicily is a galley and so is the 'horse ship' (*hippagogus*) in the mosaic at Althiburus in Tunisia. But no matter how carefully the ships were prepared and equipped, only a very small percentage of animals reached Rome alive. The journey from the ports of Carthage, Leptis Magna, Alexandria, Caesarea and Antioch must have been a time of unimaginable torment for them. During the long voyage many succumbed to self-inflicted wounds in their tight cages, to illness brought on by unfamiliar food, or to mistreatment by impatient keepers. And then there were often delays caused by having to sail against the prevailing north-westerly wind. The journey from

Carthage, on the north coast of Africa, to Rome took four to six days, from Alexandria or Antioch around a month, but the ships could be repeatedly delayed by storms.

Hippopotamuses and crocodiles were probably the least able to cope with the deprivations of the crossing. It is safe to assume, of course, that the Romans did little to reproduce the animals' native environment during the crossing, unlike the directors of European zoos in the nineteenth century. Victorian animal collectors wanted to keep their hippos in good condition, so they transported them in special tanks three-quarters full of water to keep their temperature as low as possible. The Romans did have ships with wooden wells in them, designed to keep fish catches alive, but it seems unlikely they could have adapted these to the needs of very large amphibious creatures. In any case, the Romans had different plans for these animals. They were not interested in their welfare at all. Everyone knew from the start that most of the animals would not live long once they reached Rome. They would generally appear only once, as special attractions. So if they died on the journey, it was merely part of a calculated financial risk, and a new transport would be organised in the emperor's name.

It was always quite a job to get an elephant weighing more than 3,000 kilos to board a large cargo ship. A fourth-century mosaic in a house in Veii shows an elephant carefully making its way along a gangplank. Two cables have been attached to its legs, held taut by four men on shore and four men on the ship to prevent the animal from losing its balance. Given the size and weight of an elephant it is hard to believe that more than three or four of these animals could have been

Mosaic at Veii showing an elephant being led on to a ship

transported on a ship measuring little more than 40 metres. It cannot have been easy when the ship started rolling and heaving on the waves. The people tending the animals must have needed all the persuasiveness they could muster to keep them calm. The hardest test of all came when it was time to disembark. Pliny the Elder[110] describes the trouble some keepers once went to as they tried to get their elephants ashore at Puteoli. They led the elephants to the gangplank, but the distance between them and the quayside terrified the elephants so much that they refused to take another step. In the end the men managed to persuade the elephants to allow themselves to be led off the ship backwards, so that they were not forced to look at the gap they still had to cross.

Most of the ships heading for Rome would moor in the harbour at Ostia. From there the wild animals were brought into the city on large carts or on special river craft called *codiciariae*. The elephants probably walked the last 30 kilometres or so, led by their keepers. In Rome all the animals were housed in special zoos (*vivaria*), either on the Campus Martius, a short distance away in the gardens of the imperial palaces, or just outside the city. The night before a gladiator show the whole of Rome must have echoed to the sad and ghastly howling of distressed animals, and the rumbling of carts rattling over the cobbles, transporting them to the dark cages beneath the Colosseum. There they would wait for the inevitable, their one and only performance in the arena. They were given precisely the right amount of food to ensure that they would do what they had been brought there to do: charge ferociously towards the other animals or human victims, living creatures deliberately exposed to their teeth and claws.

A Day at the Colosseum

And now they have to pay; they give them games
And if the people turn their thumbs down and
demand a blood bath, they're happy to provide
them with one.[111]

Juvenal

As the date of a gladiator show approached, walls all over the city were plastered with posters. These were usually attractively painted advertisements with written information about why the games were being held and how many gladiators and wild animals were scheduled to appear. Several of these placards have been found in Pompeii, one of which reads:

> Twenty pairs of gladiators owned by D. Lucretius Sater Valens, lifelong priest to Nero Caesar Augustus, and ten pairs of gladiators owned by his son D. Lucretius Valens, will engage in combat in Pompeii on the 8th, 9th, 10th, 11th, and 12th of April. There will also be wild animal hunts, as permitted by law. The seats will be shaded with awnings.[112]

We do not know the price of a ticket for 'a day at the Colosseum', but it was probably more than most Romans could afford. People from the lower orders nevertheless came in large numbers, simply because either the emperor, the sponsor, or a rich senator keen to assume the role of patron, had decided to make free tickets available. These must have been distributed in much the same way as tickets for a mass hunting event organised by Caligula in the Circus Maximus to celebrate his sister Drusilla's wedding. The night before the performance he hinted that free tickets might be available. Thousands of people rushed to where the tickets were handed out, hoping it might be their lucky day. People must have been even more eager to see a spectacular gladiator fight in the Colosseum than to see a show in the Circus Maximus, since fights were much less frequent than chariot races, and the Circus Maximus could take as many as 200,000 spectators, as opposed to only 50,000 in the Colosseum.

The standard programme for a day at the Colosseum had an established sequence of events. In the morning there were animal fights, immediately followed by the wild animal hunts (*venationes*). Criminals and absconding slaves were executed at lunchtime, sometimes with light-hearted interludes, such as comic turns and competitive athletics. The main feature was saved for the afternoon: the gladiator fights.

The whole programme lasted for many hours and it would be satisfying to be able to describe it from beginning to end, the way a sports commentator follows a match minute by minute, but this is not possible since we simply do not have enough information. We have to content ourselves with fragmentary reports by the authors of the day. They do write about the amazing fights and describe the heady atmosphere in the arena, and they make no secret of their sympathies and antipathies. They are full of admiration when a gladiator looks death fearlessly in the face in his final moments, but they do not give any blow-by-blow accounts of exciting fights, let alone a report of a whole day at the Colosseum. Only Martial, whom I have already quoted several times, enters fully into the spirit of things. But in his *Book of Spectacles* (*Liber de Spectaculis*) he concentrates on specific details and abstract observations, and he writes more about fights between men and animals than actual gladiatorial combat. The other writers are all outsiders, providing information about a world in which they did not feel at home. We have to connect up the random references made by various different authors and set these alongside images of fights in frescoes, mosaics and reliefs. If we study these images closely, we see that visual artists were better able to make the leap of imagination necessary to depict the world of the Colosseum than writers were. They reveal the power, the vulnerability and terrible despair of the gladiators with an enormous sense of drama. Most depictions are snapshots: a fully armed gladiator as the supreme victor, or a defeated man living out his last desperate moments; a wild animal leaping at its prey or being fatally attacked.

One mosaic stands out from all the rest: the Zliten mosaic, named after the place in Libya where it was found, not far from the ancient town of Leptis Magna. We do not know its date, which could be anything from the end of the first century AD to the beginning of the third. It was originally laid out in a villa belonging to a rich man who wanted to see an entire gladiator show depicted in his own home. The images around the edge of this astonishing mosaic, which measures 4 by 3.5 metres, represent the entire day's programme of a gladiator show. We see the hunting of wild animals, animal fights, executions and gladiatorial combat.

Part of the Zliten mosaic showing an opening procession
and gladiator fights

The Morning Programme: Hunting and
Animal Fights

The atmosphere in the Colosseum is quite terrifying,
even at dawn. As thousands of spectators make their
way to their seats, they can hear the trumpeting of
elephants, the howling and barking of dogs and wolves,
and the roars of lions and tigers coming from the cages
beneath the arena. Finally, the moment arrives when the
lift cages are winched up and the animals run out
through the narrow gangways that lead up to the
trapdoors giving on to the arena. Sometimes the cages
are placed in the niches in the podium wall before the
show starts and the animals are freed into the arena
from there. No one knows for certain whether they will
rush enthusiastically into the arena or become skittish
when suddenly surrounded by a cheering crowd and

bright daylight after so many hours of darkness. There are reports that some wild animals freeze with shock and become quite apathetic, cowering in corners. But there are always the keepers whipping them into action. They wave bunches of burning straw or red-hot iron bars at them, poking and prodding them.

The morning programme is divided into three parts: first the animal fights, then circus acts and finally the hunt. The order in which the animal fights take place is never announced beforehand. The programme posters show which animals will be involved but not in which combinations. The Zliten mosaic mentioned earlier shows one possible combination. A bear and a bull have been tied together with a chain and a rope. A naked man, possibly sentenced to be killed by wild animals, rushes towards them with a hook to separate the two creatures. Once he has done this, there will be a fight to the death. The combination of bear and bull is a frequent one, because it guarantees a spectacular confrontation.

Part of the Zliten mosaic showing a fight between a bear and a bull

Even more spectacular are the fights Martial describes: a bull against an elephant, a lion against a leopard, a rhinoceros against a buffalo. The animal that emerges victorious at the end of the fight cannot count on a reprieve though. If it does not succumb to its wounds, the hunters kill it, unless it is one of the few animals still fit enough to be used again the next day.

When the organisers of the games feel the audience has seen enough of this sort of fight, they send on well-trained, tame animals to provide more frivolous entertainment in the arena. Boys dance on the backs of bulls, elephants perform dance routines, walk the tightrope or dine in the arena. Meticulously trained leopards, tigers, bears and wild boars imitate gladiator fights, wearing what is supposed to look like armour. The climax is the 'victory over nature'. Rabbits or hares are let loose into the arena and chased by trained lions, tigers or dogs. This is not really a hunt at all but a game. A predator picks up a hare, lets it go again and then snatches it up in its jaws and delivers it to its keeper completely unharmed.

Things can sometimes go wrong for a trained predator when a large prey, such as a bear, suddenly turns on its attacker, taking it by surprise and fatally mauling it. Statius (late first-century poet) tells the story of a tame lion that, to the great distress of the crowd, forgets its natural hunting instinct and becomes the victim of an enraged animal that has already turned and fled:

> What have you gained by throwing off your wild
>   instincts,
> Becoming tame, forgetting how to kill criminals,
> Tolerating authority, serving a lesser being?

What did it profit you to leave your pen and meekly
    return
Back to your cell, to catch prey and let it go again
Or tolerate hands inside your muzzle with slack
    jaws?
You are dead, marvellous plunderer of mighty prey.
Not because, hunted down and surrounded,
Stirred to ghastly anger, you leapt towards the spears
In Africa or were tricked by a trap.
You were defeated by a fleeing animal. Sadly your
    cage
Stands here wide open; all around, behind closed
    gates,
The docile lions roared that such an outrage was
    allowed.
As they watched you being dragged away, their
    manes
Drooped with shame, a frown darkened their eyes.
Yet that strange disgrace did not overwhelm you
With the first blow: your will stayed strong, your
    courage returned,
Even as you were slipping into death your threats
Remained forceful. Like a heavily wounded soldier
Who deliberately walks towards his enemy, half dead –
he raises his arm, brandishes his sword, which falls
    from his hand . . .
So he walked: slowly, without his former radiance, a
    fixated look,
Mouth open, panting after his enemy and for air.
Defeated and abruptly killed, you still have
One great comfort: the senate and the people
    mourned
When you died, as if a beloved gladiator

Had fallen in the cruel sand. The great Emperor,
With so many animals from Egypt, the Rhine delta,
From Africa and Scythia, that no one grieves for,
Has been touched by the absence of one lost lion.[113]

The 'victory of the emperor over nature' leads up to
the next item on the programme, the *venatio*, men and
animals in head-on combat. The main roles here are
reserved for the hunters (*venatores*) and for the men
who fight wild animals (*bestiarii*). In the second and
first centuries BC they are barely distinguishable from
other gladiators, with their metal helmets, leg-plates and
swords. But when the hunting events and gladiator
fights start to be held in the same amphitheatre on the
same day – from the beginning of the imperial period –
they take to wearing nothing except a sort of tunic, with
protective strapping around their legs, and to fighting
with their hunting spears only. In the second century
their equipment changes again: they don a kind of
breast armour and fight with a sword and a shield.

The *venatio* begins with a mass chase after animals
that are not dangerous at all. Large numbers of ostriches,
antelope, gazelles, deer and donkeys are herded into the
arena and killed. Before long the arena floor is red with
blood and strewn with hundreds of corpses. Stable
hands rush out to clear up everything and replace the
dirty sand. As soon as the arena looks presentable again
the next round of slaughter begins. But this time the
animal victims are savage beasts, 'lords of the wilder-
ness': bears, tigers, leopards, lions and elephants. The
fights always end with the slaying of the animals, but
occasionally a hunter is killed by an enraged predator.
Either way, the floor is swept clean and more animals

Cast of a relief from the Villa Torlonia showing huntsmen
fighting a lion, a panther and a bear

are chased into the arena. This goes on until midday.

There was no limit to how far some emperors would go in their efforts to enhance the entertainment value of these events. In AD 203 Septimius Severus thought up a particularly memorable act for the festivities to mark his first ten years as emperor. He had scenery constructed that transformed the arena into a kind of giant boat with 400 animals waiting inside it. At a signal from the emperor a shipwreck was staged. It looked as if an invisible force was breaking the boat apart so that all the 'passengers' tumbled out. Suddenly the arena was full of bears, bison, panthers, lionesses, wild donkeys and ostriches, running around at random. Then the huntsmen appeared and chased and killed all the animals to great cheers from the crowd.[114]

To the Romans, the slaughter of all these animals was further proof of civilised Rome's domination over uncivilised nature. Nevertheless there must have been moments when even the most die-hard fans of the Colosseum began to tire of all the violence and to feel sorry for the desperate animals. Two occasions in particular come to mind. The first was a hunting event with wild swine. Three fragments of verse by Martial describe what happened:

> In the fierce tumult of Caesar's hunting party
> a pregnant swine was hit with a lightweight lance
> and a premature piglet poked out of the mother's lap.
> How cruel you are Lucina.[115] You call this 'breeding'?
> The animal would rather have died of its many
>   wounds,
> and then every one of her young would have seen the
>   light.
> Bacchus too had life only thanks to his mother's death.
> A god came into the world this way and now an animal
>   as well.

> Mortally injured, heavily wounded, the sow was forced
> to lose life and give it at the same time.
> How accurately, how precisely the target was hit:
> it was definitely Lucina's doing.
> The dying creature experienced Diana's twofold ·
>   power:
> as a mother it was liberated, as an animal killed.

> A pregnant swine, its stomach laden with young,
> was heavily wounded, which made a mother of her.
> The sow gave birth and fell, the little piglet ran off.
> See here another strange case of happenstance.[116]

Death bringing forth new life like that must have made people think. And another incident evoked an emotional response. It is mentioned by three writers, Seneca, Pliny the Elder and Cassius Dio[117] and it happened during the great games organised by Pompey in the Circus Maximus in 55 BC. Twenty elephants were being chased by Gaetuli, intrepid African tribal huntsmen. When the Gaetuli had killed a number of them the rest did what no one had thought possible. They ganged up and charged the men attacking them, tossed their shields in the air with their trunks and stormed on towards the high wall that had been built to protect the spectators. They trumpeted so furiously that everyone panicked. The authors have an explanation for this terrifying performance. It was said that just before they were put on the ships that would bring them to Rome, the elephants, who are loyal creatures capable of becoming attached to their keepers in a relationship of blind trust, were promised by those who were to accompany them on the voyage that not a hair on their heads would be harmed. Here in the arena they discovered that the promise had been broken, and they made their sense of outrage very clear. Far from proving insensitive to the despairing sound of trumpeting elephants, the crowd began to reproach Pompey, the organiser of the show. Were people simply frightened, or did they feel sorry for the elephants? It was probably a combination of the two. The hunting event was abandoned. This did not help the elephants very much, for a few days later they were all killed anyway.

Later in this morning's programme there will also be individual events featuring the *venatores* and the *bestiarii*. There are two different acts, the first is not

Second-century relief showing bullfighters

unlike a rodeo. An unarmed huntsman will mount a horse and ride towards a bull, jump from his horse on to the bull, grab the bull by the horns and try to push it to the ground and strangle it to death. Naturally there is always a risk he will come off worst. Huntsmen who take on lions, tigers or bears armed only with spears are at even greater risk. Sometimes the tormented animals tear their attackers to pieces, but the huntsmen usually win. Even a victorious hunter cannot necessarily take comfort in a successful outcome, however. If the crowd jeer he will know that his performance has not satisfied them and he is going to be sent out for a second fight. There is a good chance the exhausted huntsman will be killed the second time round.

Although the *venatores* and *bestiarii* did not generally inspire much respect, a few of them did attain high status, that ranked alongside the most successful gladiators. The most famous of these was Carpophorus. Nothing is known of his background except that he came from the north; he may have been a captured German condemned to perform in the arena. He emerged as a fearless fighter who took on bears and lions. Martial speaks very enthusiastically about his performances and mentions several of his exploits:

From his firm hand, lance after lance goes straight to its
   target:
Carpophorus is young but massively strong.
He once carried two bulls on his shoulders as if they
   weighed nothing
and he has defeated a buffalo and a bison.
Yes, a lion was afraid of him and allowed itself to be
   cornered!
So come on, people, grumble "It's taking so long!"[118]

Martial even has the audacity to compare him with the
mythical heroes Meleager and Hercules, both of whom
became famous for killing large animals:

The act Meleager thought of as the high point of his
   career
turned out to be a trivial task for Carpophorus:
The killing of a boar. His lance also speared
a bear from the high north, a very dangerous creature.
He floored an enormous lion too, which would not
have looked out of place in Hercules' heroic hands,
And he showed no mercy to a truly breathtaking
   leopard. And even then,
after so many victories, he was still able to fight on.[119]

The Interval Attractions: Executions

You might have thought that by lunchtime the spectators will want a bit of a break from watching
bloodthirsty violence and will leave their seats to get
something to eat and to rest for a while. A number of
them do feel like a break and leave the arena, only
returning when the gladiator fights proper are about to

start. But there are plenty more who do not want to miss any of the events that take place during the interval. In some cases this is because they have free tickets and are afraid of losing their seats, but others are unable to tear themselves away, like Emperor Claudius, who seldom if ever leaves his box at lunchtime and clearly enjoys watching the public execution of criminals.

The evening before their execution, closely packed together on carts, the condemned prisoners are brought to the Colosseum from all over the city and herded into the dark, stinking cells under the arena. Some are feeling such despair that they do not wait for execution and decide to end their lives themselves. Seneca tells of one slave who suddenly sticks his head through one of the wheels of the cart taking him to the Colosseum. His head is crushed, but at least he is spared the humiliation of a painful, ignominious death watched by an enthralled and hostile crowd.[120] The rest spend their last night crowded together in cramped cells. Around midday they are brought up from their underground cells and divided into two groups, Roman citizens on one side, non-citizens and slaves on the other. The slaves have to wait. First to be executed are Roman citizens with murder on their conscience.

For citizens it will at least be a relatively quick death by the sword (*ad gladium*). Non-citizens are sentenced to death on the cross (*crucifixio*), by fire (*crematio* or *ad flammas*) or by wild animals (*ad bestias*).[121] These public executions are not motivated by sadism alone. Carrying out these sentences in public is one more way for the authorities to reinforce prevailing social relationships. Criminals, especially the slaves among them, have crossed a boundary. By committing their crimes (murder, desecration of the temple and arson are mentioned) they have put themselves in a position where reparations will be demanded of them and severe punishment seen as justified. Public humiliation followed by death in full view of the people of Rome is the price they pay.

The execution of citizens can be quite simple: a single blow from an executioner's sword. But there are other ways it can be staged, ways more appropriate to the atmosphere of a day at the Colosseum. Two condemned men may be sent into the arena together, one armed with a sword, the other unarmed and dressed only in a loincloth. Naturally enough, the unarmed man runs away. The man with the sword pursues him and eventually stabs him to death. Once he has accomplished this he is forced to surrender his sword. Then he in turn is chased and killed by another prisoner. This goes on until only one man is left and he is killed by a *venator* or a *bestiarius*. Citizens are occasionally crucified along with slaves, which is regarded as an additional humiliation. Once, when a citizen who had been sentenced to death in Spain complained to Governor Galba, later to become emperor, that he as a Roman citizen should not have to share the fate of slaves, Galba was unimpressed by his protest and ordered the executioners to hang him on a higher cross.

The execution of citizens is a prelude to the execution of non-citizens and slaves. A final procession of condemned slaves into the middle of the arena is portrayed in a marble relief from Smyrna, now in the Ashmolean Museum in Oxford. Helmeted men hold on to a rope that runs through the metal collar around each condemned man's neck. Ravenous wild animals are then let loose to tear the poor slaves apart.

Final procession of condemned slaves

Christian writers have left detailed information about these midday executions. Their accounts of the execution of their fellow believers are very vivid: Christians were condemned to a harrowing and painful death for refusing to worship the emperor as a god. Some even write of their own longing for martyrdom in one of the Roman arenas. One of the most famous of these martyrs is Ignatius of Antioch. At the beginning of the second century he was taken to the Colosseum in Rome to be thrown to wild animals. In his *Letter to the Romans* he describes his feelings about his approaching death and the torments that await him there:

From Syria to Rome, day and night, on land and sea, I fight wild animals, chained as I am to ten leopards, by which I mean a unit of soldiers. If you are good to them, they get even more vicious. But I suffer their ill treatment, I become even more resolved in my discipleship, but that cannot wipe out my sense of blame. I hope I will enjoy the wild animals that are being kept ready for me and I pray they will set upon me quickly. And I will excite them so that they eat me in the shortest possible time, and so avoid the way it goes with some people when the animals are afraid of them and refuse to touch them. And if they are unmoved I will force them. Forgive me, I know what is good for me. Only now am I beginning my discipleship. Do not let any visible or invisible being try to stop me going to Jesus Christ out of jealousy. Fire and crucifixion, packs of wild animals, slashing, tearing, ripping me to pieces, splintering bones, dislocating limbs, crushing my whole body: let me suffer the worst torments of the devil, so long as I may go to Jesus Christ.[122]

Ignatius' desire for a martyr's death is a phenomenon encountered repeatedly in Christian literature. The martyrs and their supporters did not care whether they were killed by wild beasts, hung on the cross, or were burnt to death, as long as they got into the Kingdom of Heaven.

Sometimes the Romans combined different kinds of death penalty: a condemned man might be nailed to a cross and then burnt, or hanged in such a way that wild animals could tear at his limbs. A number of different mosaics show what could be done to him. In the Zliten mosaic a guard is dragging a victim towards the wild animals, a man tied to a post on a long-handled, two-wheeled cart. The mosaic at the Domus Sollertiana in El Djem in Tunisia presents a similar scene: two prisoners, barefoot, their hands tied at their waists, are surrounded by wild animals on the attack. The face of one of the victims is hidden by a leopard that has already begun mauling it, the wide open eyes of another show his terror as he confronts the predators' raised claws. A little terracotta figurine, also from North Africa, depicts a particularly distressing scene. A woman sits astride a bull. She is naked apart from a loincloth and her hands are tied behind her back. The bull is already down on its knees and a leopard is tearing at the woman's breast (see page 155).

Seneca described the executions as massacres *sine arte*, without any artistry, which really meant that he could not understand why so many people should stare goggle-eyed at these interval acts, when they were neither more nor less than crude slaughter. Perhaps even the crowd found the executions monotonous, too predictable, and perhaps this is why the organisers sometimes provided the executions with a mythological

Sections of the mosaic at the Domus Sollertiana, El Djem
(Tunisia), showing the execution of condemned prisoners

framework. The execution would be dressed up as a
narrative, with the condemned men taking part in a play
to arouse the audience's curiosity. A favourite way of
making these interval executions more exciting was to
use famous myths that ended with the death of the main
character. This made the executions more effective as

drama and the spectators' attention could be held for longer. Another consideration may have been to make a symbolic representation of the boundary between the normal and the abnormal. By making condemned prisoners play a leading role in dramatised versions of fatal myths, the emperor could once more demonstrate his absolute authority and his power over life and death.

One myth was repeatedly re-enacted. This was the 'execution' of Orpheus, the musician who enchanted both men and animals with his playing and singing. After the death of his beloved Eurydice, he descended into the underworld, where Hades gave him permission to lead her back to the land of the living. But he lost her again when he broke their agreement by looking round at her. Overcome with sorrow, he is said to have withdrawn from the world and renounced all women, ultimately being torn to pieces by Thracian women. This fate was played out in the Colosseum, except that the killers were not maddened women but wild beasts that attacked Orpheus as he lay tied to a rock in the amphitheatre. Martial gives us an impression of one performance:

> Everything that was ever seen of Orpheus in the
>   mountains
> has been presented to you here, Caesar.
> Rocks, miraculous woods slid closer,
> complete with golden apples.
> Among the fowls, savage beasts roamed free
> and birds hovered around the singer's head.
> But all this, it seems, was lost on one particular bear,
>   and Orpheus
> was torn apart: so what was once painted has now
>   actually happened. [123]

Another story, that Martial[124] claims was acted out in the arena, was that of Pasiphae and the bull. Minos, King of Crete, was given a bull as a gift by the god Poseidon. When he added it to his herds rather than sacrificing it, Poseidon set Minos' wife Pasiphae ablaze with love for the animal. To satisfy her lusts she arranged to conceal herself in a cunning replica of a heifer. The bull reciprocated her love, which resulted in the birth of the Minotaur, half-man, half-bull. In the arena, a woman prisoner would be draped with a cowhide and her vagina smeared with blood from a cow on heat. Martial

Terracotta figurine showing the execution of a woman tied to a bull

does not provide any details of this violent coupling, but we can assume that the woman would have been horribly degraded and badly maimed before she was brutally put to death.

Sometimes criminals were dressed up as mythological figures without any effort being made to reflect the myth with any degree of accuracy. The story of Daedalus left plenty of scope for inventive interpretations, because little was known about this architect of the Labyrinth, except that he had attached wings to himself and his son Icarus and had flown off into the sky over Crete. Martial[125] says that when Daedalus was killed by a bear, he was no longer wearing the wings that had carried him safely away from Crete. We can conclude from this that the victim would probably have worn wings at the start of the performance that were taken from him at the end, after which he was lowered into a bear's cage by means of some sort of winch mechanism.

Sometimes criminals were forced to play famous villains, whose punishment had taken on a mythological slant. The Laureolus story is particularly well known. After committing a series of crimes Laureolus was put to death in the arena in a particularly gruesome manner. After this, his death was repeatedly re-enacted, each time in different circumstances. Martial describes one such performance:

> Just as Prometheus, chained to his rock,
> feeds a bird with the plentiful flesh of his breast,
> So did Laureolus nailed to a cross, no longer mere
>   décor but the living truth,
> Offer a Scottish bear his stomach,

His body became a bloody heap of tatters:
living, yes, but no longer human.
His punishment was just. The villain had cut the throat
of his lord or overlord, or reached out
his desecrating hands for ancient temple gold, or
    abandoned
you, Rome, to cruel flames!
His deeds put all myths in the shade.
And his punishment as well: an old story come true.[126]

Whichever story is chosen and however opportunistically the dénouement is framed, it is still a matter of waiting to see whether the animals will be willing to co-operate and produce a real spectacle. The animals may be sick, overwhelmed by the noise or simply not hungry, which can be far from satisfactory for the people who thought up these acts, especially when a temperamental emperor and a dissatisfied crowd make their displeasure heard at the tops of their voices. Heathen writers refer to this kind of eventuality with an attitude of 'that's simply the way it goes sometimes', but when Christian authors report on the martyrdom of their fellow believers they present one obvious explanation for an outcome like this: the martyrs' innocence. When Tertullian[127] writes about the sufferings of the holy Perpetua and Felicitas he describes how, in the arena at Carthage one of Perpetua's companions, Saturus, was tied to a wild boar. Things did not turn out the way everyone had been anticipating. The boar did drag its prey around with it, but it refused to sink its teeth into the victim. Instead it attacked the *bestiarius* who had accompanied it into the arena and killed him. The organisers were furious. They tied Saturus' arms to a frame and set a bear on him. But the animal refused to come out if its cage. Only on a third attempt did they achieve the desired result. A leopard tore Saturus to pieces. The frustration of the audience was so great that, after revelling in his suffering, they demanded that his throat be sliced open immediately for everyone to see, rather than waiting until the dead man had been taken away to an area specially equipped for that purpose.

Once, probably during a show put on by Augustus, something truly remarkable happened. Androclus, a condemned slave from Dacia, was placed in the middle of the arena. The gates were pulled up and a lion charged out. But instead of attacking the unfortunate slave it wagged its tail, lay down in front of him and licked his feet. The organiser of the games was maddened with rage and sent a leopard into the arena. The lion immediately turned on the leopard and killed it. The organiser called the slave over to him. Androclus told him that he had run away from his callous master, the Governor of Africa, and hidden deep in the interior of the country in an abandoned cave. One day a lion appeared. Androclus thought his final hour had come, but the lion only moaned and showed him a wounded paw with a large thorn embedded in it that was causing an infection. He extracted the thorn and treated the paw. Out of gratitude the lion brought him meat every day. He survived for some time that way, but eventually he was tracked down by the governor's soldiers. His master sentenced him to death by wild animals and here in the arena in Rome he had come upon the very lion he once cared for. It too had been caught and brought to the Colosseum. The story ended with both Androclus and the lion being given their freedom.[128]

The sequel to the executions is a scene of mytho-logical drama, according to Tertullian, our authority on the matter. Walking among the corpses strewn in the arena is a remarkable character. His nose does not look human at all, but more like a bird's beak. He is dressed in tight-fitting clothes and wears leather shoes with pointed toes. In his hand he holds a large, long-handled hammer. He represents the ferryman Charon, who transports the dead across the River Styx to the under-world. This is a figure based on the Etruscan god of death, also called Charon, and alongside him stands the god Mercury in his role of accompanying human souls. With the burning point of his staff, Mercury jabs the victims' flesh to make sure they are really dead. Then Charon takes possession of each body and hits it with his hammer. After this ritual, the bodies are dragged out of the arena by Colosseum staff with large hooks.[129]

The Afternoon Programme: Gladiator Fights

By early afternoon all the spectators are back in their seats. While the arena is being cleaned and the bodies hauled away, they sit waiting for the *pompa*, the solemn ceremonial procession that marks the official start of the gladiator fights. As far as the spectators are concerned, the performance really started one or two days earlier, when all the participants were presented to the public in the Roman Forum. One by one the gladiators were led out in front of the crowd. The public was told how old each of them was, where he came from, which weapons he fought with, how many fights he had survived, and how many victories he already had to his name. A written programme was produced at this

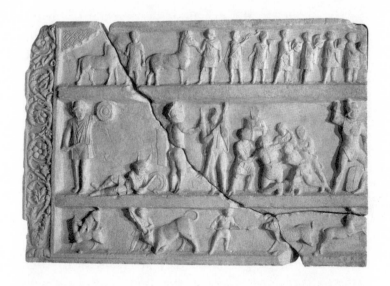

Relief on a grave dating from AD 20-30 depicting gladiator games in Pompeii, showing procession, gladiatorial combat and a hunt

point, stating who would fight whom. Some of the crowd would also have been present at the banquet (*cena libera*) held for the gladiators by the sponsor on the evening before the performance. It must have felt strange standing face to face with the gladiators as they tucked into what might be their last meal. There was an element of voyeurism too. The guests were witnesses to a meal that symbolised the boundary between life and death. The next day several of their fellow diners would no longer be alive.

The silence is palpable as the opening ceremony begins. A long procession walks up out of the passage-ways under the arena. A relief on the grave of a Pompeii city official (*c*. AD 20-30) shows this solemn opening

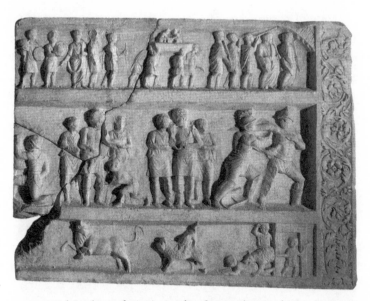

procession (see above). At the front, dressed in togas, are two *lictors*, servants of the organiser of the games (*munerarius*). They are carrying *fasces* over their shoulders, bundles of sticks representing their master's power. Behind them are the trumpeters (*tubicines*). They are followed by four men carrying a litter, on which sit two blacksmiths, their presence a guarantee that the gladiators' weapons are in order. Next in line are two people, one with a *tabella*, a writing tablet giving further information about the fights, the other with an olive branch for the winner. Behind them is the organiser himself, in a toga, followed by six servants holding the gladiators' shields and helmets. Then comes another man with a trumpet, in this case a curved horn (*cornu*). At the rear of the procession are two servants leading a horse that would have been used by a mounted gladiator. This Pompeian relief is a rather modest representation of the initial procession. In provincial towns the numbers taking part could easily have reached several dozens, and in the Colosseum many times that, since the gladiators themselves, not shown in the relief, would also have joined the parade.

In the middle of the arena the procession comes to a halt. Is this for an official inspection of the weapons, as the relief suggests by showing shields and helmets being carried in as well? This is certainly possible, but because no offensive weapons are included, it seems more likely that the gladiators have removed their helmets and shields so that everyone can admire the beauty of their unclad athletic bodies. A band plays continually as they make their entrance into the arena, with trumpeters, horn players and double flutes (*tibiae*). In the Zliten mosaic (see page 138) a water organ is shown as well, with wooden pipes, played by a woman sitting at what looks like a desk.

As soon as the procession has gone back down into the depths of the amphitheatre, the gladiators' 'warm-up' begins, known to the Romans as the 'overture'. Two by two, in pairs chosen by the organiser and the gladiator manager, the gladiators enter the arena and start mock battles with wooden weapons, probably the ones they had used in training. This gives them a chance to stretch their muscles and get the public into the right mood for the real fights.

At a signal from the chief umpire, the gladiators leave the arena again and the real weapons, the 'sharp irons' (*ferra acuta*), are carried into the arena and officially tested. The blades are inspected and sharpened if necessary. When it comes to ensuring that the fight will be as lethal as possible, nothing at all is left to chance.

As the first pair of gladiators enters the arena, the

orchestra plays stirring, rhythmic music. It is a wide-spread misconception that all gladiators, as they passed the emperor's box to greet him, uttered the words 'Hail, Caesar, those who are about to die salute you' (*Ave Caesar, morituri te salutant*). Suetonius,[130] the source of this expression, tells us only that, during a 'sea battle' organised by Emperor Claudius on Lake Fucino, the 9,000 prisoners, who had the leading roles, were said to have greeted the emperor with these words (see page 179). But there is no suggestion that gladiators would have said anything of the kind. Nor is it likely, since gladiators went into a fight in the hope of winning and surviving, like Roman soldiers facing difficult battle situations.

Right from the start of the fight, people in the crowd make themselves heard. They are not simply enthusiastic spectators, cheering or jeering, but to some degree are also participants in each fight, since they may be involved in the final outcome. They are aware that a moment may arrive when their voices can make the difference between life and death. People who in normal life are completely powerless and dependent on the goodwill of the emperor are given an unfamiliar sense of power by the knowledge that they may hold another man's life in their hands here in the arena.

But before it comes to that, the two gladiators fight a ferocious battle. All the tricks they have learnt in their long training are now put into practice. They switch between defence and attack, make dummy moves, parry and dodge thrusts, seek out the vulnerable parts of their opponent's body, use the advantage of surprise. Blind thrusts are suicidal, because the gladiator managers have put these two particular men up against each other to

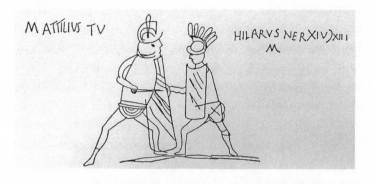

M ATTILIVS TV

HILARVS NER XIV)XIII
M

MATT

M ATTILIVS I)I
V

L RAECIVS FELIX
XII)X II · M

Graffiti from Pompeii showing Attilius' victory

produce an exciting fight, believing they are well matched. Opponents often know each other and are aware of each other's strengths and weaknesses. Young novices are rarely made to fight experienced veterans, but sometimes the gladiator manager has no choice other than to send a youthful, inexperienced fighter into the ring against an old stager. The young gladiator does not always come off badly. Graffiti in Pompeii[131] show that a novice, if he is endowed with enough natural talent, definitely has a chance of winning. The gifted gladiator in the picture is Marcus Attilius, unknown on the circuit. He fights as a *murmillo* against Hilarus, a *thraex* with fourteen victories to his name, and he wins. Both the emperor and the public enjoy the fight. Attilius receives his prize to thunderous applause and Hilarus is allowed to leave the arena alive. With this victory, Attilius makes an instant name for himself and is once more put up against an experienced *thraex*. We know this from a further piece of graffiti,[132] which depicts his victory over another veteran, Lucius Raecius Felix, who has achieved victory twelve times. This *thraex* also has to admit defeat, only getting away with his life thanks to the verdict of the emperor and the people.

The way a gladiator must have felt as he entered the arena to confront an opponent generally regarded as stronger than himself is saliently described by the rhetorician Quintilian:

> The day had dawned, people had already gathered for the spectacle of our punishment, the bodies of the condemned men had already been displayed and now they were made to walk across the arena in a death parade. Our owner, who wanted to win popularity by spilling our blood, was ready. However, one aspect of my situation aroused the compassion of some of those present, as can happen when a person is randomly thrown into the arena and no one knows anything about his fate, or about his sons or his father; I seemed to have too strong an opponent, I was certain to fall victim, to collapse on the sand, no one was cheaper than I was in the organiser's eyes. The instruments of death could be heard everywhere: one man was sharpening a sword, another was heating metal plates in a fire [the plates used to prevent the gladiators leaving the arena], in one area truncheons

were being laid ready, in another whips. Then the bassoons let forth their sinister sounds, stretchers were carried in from the mortuary and a funeral procession took place before anyone had died. Wounds, death rattles and blood were everywhere.[133]

Although little is known about the rules of the game, we can take it that both the gladiators and the audience know what is allowed and what is not. In depictions of the games we sometimes see an umpire, dressed in a tunic and carrying a wooden staff, watching a fight closely. Perhaps he is there to make sure a frightened gladiator stays within the clearly marked chalk boundaries and does not flee in panic across the arena as he tries to avoid the fatal thrust of a superior opponent. No doubt the umpire would intervene repeatedly if both opponents decide to abandon the fight, whether from apathy or exhaustion. He spurs them to greater activity, sometimes using the searing hot metal plates mentioned by Quintilian.

It is impossible to predict how long a fight may last. If the gladiators can hold their own against each other and neither one of them manages to force an outcome, a fight may continue for a very long time. The spectators passionately support their favourite, cheering him on and trying to scream him to victory. If both gladiators begin to look close to exhaustion without a winner emerging, the umpire will step in and declare a short break to let them catch their breath and quench their thirst. If the fight resumes and still neither man seems about to win, he stops them. He then turns to the emperor and the public to ask them for their verdict. Gladiators who have fought bravely are granted an honourable exit. *Stantes missi* (sent away standing) is the official term. Gladiators must have been proud of undecided contests, since they are mentioned in grave inscriptions alongside victories. Martial describes one inconclusive fight:

> Priscus managed to draw out the fight. Versus too,
> and their strengths remained well matched.
> 'Enough now, both may go!' the cry went up
>   repeatedly
> but Caesar stuck firmly to his own law
> (the law that states: fight until one submits),
> although he did award bonuses and trophies.
> Finally the inconclusive fight came to an end.
> As they had risen together so they fell together...
> At that point Caesar had prizes brought out for both
>   fighters
> as a special reward for their courage.
> It has never happened before under any regime, my
>   emperor,
> that single combat was won by both opponents![134]

Most fights do produce a winner. One of the gladiators may succumb to exhaustion or trip over something; he may be brought down or seriously injured by a blow from his opponent or a stabbing sword thrust; in the end the balance will tip one way or the other. Many images have come down to us of that decisive moment in which a victor emerges and the loser recognises he will have to accept the *coup de grâce*. They show him kneeling in abject despair, waiting for death. The Zliten mosaic illustrates the outcome of several fights. The first is a contest between two *murmillones*. The umpire is declaring the man on the left the winner. He has just felled his opponent. The picture also shows a *retiarius* who has been gravely wounded in his leg and is appealing for mercy by sticking out his right index finger (see p. 138). Even more impressive are the highlights in the central Pompeian frieze (on p. 169). Unfortunately this frieze is not very well preserved. On the far left stands a gladiator, probably an *eques*. With his left hand he holds up his shield and in his right he grips his sword. He is on the point of killing his opponent, who is lying on the ground, still breathing, with his head raised in supplication. To his right a *thraex* also raises his sword, watched by an umpire. Next we see five men, four of them in togas and one wearing a helmet and loincloth. The helmeted man is a *thraex*. He is kneeling down, wounded, and the other four, probably amphitheatre staff, are lifting him up to carry him out of the arena. In the middle of the frieze is the most heartbreaking scene of all: two gladiators of a type hard to define (perhaps *provocatores*) are in the last stages of a fight. The man on the right has gone down on one knee and is begging the other for mercy by sticking out his left index finger. On the far right a *hoplomachus* thrusts his sword into a *murmillo's* chest. The *murmillo* can tell that it is a fatal thrust and he puts his hand to his breast in despair.

A particularly remarkable scene can be found in a fourth-century mosaic from Rome (now in the Museo Arqueologico Nacional in Madrid, see p. 170). It shows two phases of a fight. In the lower picture the *secutor* Astyanax is fighting the *retiarius* Kalendio. Kalendio has managed to throw his net over Astyanax and is threatening to finish him off with his trident. But he loses the fight after all (as seen in the upper band) because Astyanax gathers all his remaining strength and plunges his sword into Kalendio's left leg. Kalendio

A *hoplomachus* plunges his sword into a the chest of a *murmillo*. Detail from the central frieze of a grave relief, Pompeii, dating from AD 20–30

collapses and is unable to go on fighting.

Gladiators were certainly trained to die an honourable death, but it is easy to understand why some of them, staring death in the face, decided to capitulate and beg for mercy. If a man who was losing displayed his

Combat between the *secutor* Astyanax and the *retiarius*
Kalendio depicted in a fourth-century mosaic

unwillingness or inability to go on fighting by lowering
or throwing away his sword or trident, the umpire would
intervene and prevent the winner from giving the *coup
de grâce* to a defenceless opponent. He would then turn
towards the organiser of the games, who in the case of
the Colosseum was usually the emperor, and ask for his
verdict. Naturally the emperor had the power to decide
for himself, but at this point he would turn towards the
audience. This was a rare moment in which he took the
ordinary people seriously, and in that instant they had
power. They could express their opinion either by

cheering or by jeering derisively. And meanwhile the defeated gladiator would wait on his knees for the outcome. A brave fighter could hope for mercy. If he heard the cry of '*Mitte*' (let him go) or '*Missum*' (sent away), he knew he would be allowed to leave the arena alive and return to the gladiator school. A gladiator who had lost the public's sympathy would resign himself to his fate. The arena would resound to roars of '*Iugula*' (slit his throat). If he still had the strength to look up to the galleries, he would see the crowd giving the *pollice verso* (turned thumbs) signal. People pointed their thumbs up or down (exactly which of the two is still not entirely clear).[135] His fate was sealed. He was expected to die courageously. He put his arms around the torso or legs of the victor and bowed deeply. He usually kept his helmet on, so that his opponent would not be forced to look the dying man in the eye as he waited for the fatal thrust to his neck or between his shoulder blades. As he, to use the Roman jargon, 'received the iron' (*ferrum recepit*), the people shouted '*Habet, hoc habet*' (he has it).

Occasionally an emperor ignored the crowd and went against its decision by showing mercy to a defeated gladiator. The people would protest, but the emperor simply imposed his will. One day Domitian took this autonomy one step further. A fight between a *thraex* and a *murmillo* had just ended. The *murmillo* had been defeated, but the people decided he should be allowed to leave the arena with his honour intact. Domitian who, as everyone knew, was no admirer of the *thraeces*, refused to listen to the people's appeal for mercy for the loser. When one spectator commented that a *thraex* could stand up to a *murmillo* but not to the sponsor of the games, the emperor had him dragged from his seat and thrown to the dogs in the arena, with a board around his neck saying 'A friend of *thraeces*, guilty of lèse majesty'.[136]

As each fight ends, the victor walks over to the emperor's box to receive his prize of an olive branch and a sum of money, sometimes also a laurel wreath. He bows to the emperor, waves to the crowd and leaves via the Porta Sanavivaria (The Gate of Health and Life) as cheers echo around the arena. His market value has risen; from now on the sponsors will have to pay a higher price to include him in their shows. The exit of his dead opponent, carried from the field on a stretcher, must contrast starkly with his own departure, no matter how impressive the ritual surrounding the final procession in which the dead man is borne away. He is laid on a bier hung with swathes of material, representing the marriage bed of Libitina (*torus Libitinae*), the goddess of death and funerals. We cannot say for certain whether Charon and Mercury will once again act out the ritual they perform for the victims of executions. Tertullian,[137] who describes their act, believes they are present at this point. As a Christian, he

sees no real difference between the victims of the executions and the victims of the fights, since all those who die have fallen prey to Roman blood-lust. His point of view is understandable, but this particular ritual is not really relevant to the gladiator fights, where there is a very different atmosphere from that of the midday executions. It is doubtful whether there would be much enthusiasm for the scene with Charon and Mercury at this point. Probably not, because the final journey of a gladiator who has died courageously involves a great deal of respect. He is carried out of the arena through the so-called Porta Libitinaria, the Gate of Libitina. He is then taken to the *spoliarium*, a space directly adjacent to the amphitheatre where his weapons are taken from him. To be sure that he is really dead and not just faking death in order to escape, his throat is cut.

The fights continue all afternoon. Scribes employed by the Colosseum keep a careful record of events. They write a V next to the name of each victor, short for *vicit* (he has won). Next to the loser's name they write an M, the first letter of *missus* (he has been allowed to leave the arena alive), or a P for *periit* (he has perished).

Series of images in a mosaic from Verona (approximately AD 200) showing the outcome of three fights

173

Sometimes a Greek theta will appear, also known as *theta nigrum* (black theta), short for *thanatos*, the Greek word for dead. What the scribes can probably not record, but a gladiator's supporters will later immortalise in graffiti, is the term *missus periit*, meaning that after fighting bravely, the gladiator escaped death through the intervention of the emperor and the crowd, but later died of his wounds.

It is very important to the emperor that the spectators should go home feeling satisfied after a day at the Colosseum, but it is equally important for him to impress upon them that their vote in the arena does not

A fight between the *equites* Habilis and Maternus in a fourth-century mosaic

mean they have any say in events outside the Colosseum. In normal life other rules apply, so they will again be entirely dependent on him. He is their patron, the person they rely on for their material 'well-being'. This is subtly brought home to them at the end of a gladiator show, when all kinds of gifts are handed out. At the inauguration of the Colosseum, Emperor Titus was more than usually generous. Cassius Dio describes how he displayed his power and increased his popularity at the same time:

> He had small wooden balls thrown into the arena from high up in the amphitheatre, each with the name of a specific article carved into it. It might be an item of food, a piece of clothing, a silver vase or even a gold one, a horse, a beast of burden, cattle or slaves. Whoever managed to get hold of a ball had to go to the official responsible to collect the article named on it.[138]

This practice was taken up by Titus' brother Domitian and continued under subsequent emperors. It also became an established custom to share out baskets full of all kinds of delicacies after a gladiator show. This made the audience happy, because they would welcome treats however small, and the emperor would be confident that for a short time he would not have to worry about the loyalty of the people.

Sea Battles (Naumachiae)

On very special occasions, the sponsor might want to depart from the usual programme by offering some extra special attractions. At the opening of the Colosseum there were large-scale productions that drew tens of thousands of spectators, not only in the new amphitheatre but at other locations as well. Anything that seemed at all practicable was added to the programme. In spite of its brevity, Cassius Dio's description gives an idea of all the many events on offer.

Various men fought each other, in single combat but also in huge infantry battles and in naval engagements. Titus had the theatre filled with water, and horses, bulls and other tame animals were brought in and made to act in this wet element as they would do on land. He also had people sail ships in the theatre, acting out a real sea battle between the people of Corcyra [Corfu] and the Corinthians.

Others organised a similar kind of performance in the sacred forest of Gaius and Lucius, which Augustus had transformed into a lake for the purpose. On the first day there was also a gladiator show and a wild animal hunt, staged on top of the lake directly in front of the statues, where the water had been covered with a plank floor and wooden stands built up around it. On the second day there was horse racing and on the third day a sea battle with 3,000 men, followed by an infantry battle. The Athenian forces defeated those of Syracuse. They landed on an island, stormed the wall that had been built around the monument and seized it.[139]

Dio's description leaves us in no doubt that Titus' intention in holding these spectacular games on such a grand scale was to put all previous performances in the shade. His father had designed the largest amphitheatre ever built and by holding these dazzling shows Titus was trying to find an appropriate way to carry on his father's work. But Cassius Dio also hints that, even more ambitiously, Titus wanted to demonstrate to the people of Rome that no natural barrier could stand in his way, and that he, the ruler of the entire world, could even challenge the laws of nature. So he had the arena filled with water diverted by ingenious means from the Aqua Claudia and then made trained animals perform all kinds of tricks that were contrary to their natures. These circus acts were followed by a proper sea battle.

Titus was not the first to add full-scale infantry engagements and sea battles to the programme. As far as we can tell, they were introduced by Caesar. When Caesar became dictator for life in 46 BC, he put on a 'pitched battle' in the Circus Maximus about which Suetonius tells us the following:

Fights with wild animals were held for five days in a row and the whole show concluded with a battle between two armies, with 500 foot soldiers, twenty elephants, and thirty horsemen on each side. To make more space for the battle the turning posts were removed and in their place two camps were set up facing each other.[140]

Emperor Claudius added yet another dimension to the full-scale battle. He dramatised his military successes in Britain by staging the mass storming of a British town, which he had arranged to have built in replica on the Campus Martius. He led the assault himself, dressed as a general. They captured the town, unsurprisingly enough. The people of Rome cheered him on, feeling as if they themselves were participating in an event that symbolised the glory of Rome.[141]

Sea battles were part of a tradition going back to Caesar as well. To allow his victories in Gaul, Egypt, Asia Minor and North Africa to stir the imagination even further, he staged sea battles on a specially dug lake in what is now Rome's Trastevere or, again, on the Campus Martius.[142] One particular battle must have been an awe-inspiring sight. There were biremes, triremes and quadriremes with 4,000 oarsmen and 2,000 soldiers on deck in full battle dress,[143] representing the fleets of Egypt and Tyre. Based on the number of oarsmen needed for a trireme, 170, there must have been twenty-two ships, each with around ninety troops on deck. People came from far and wide to watch this spectacular event. Road intersections were blocked with tents, erected by visitors who had been unable to find accommodation in the city itself. There were even fatalities, people suffocated or were trampled to death in the crush.

This was the last spectacle of its kind at this particular venue. Three years later the lake was filled in because of the threat of epidemics. But the staging of sea battles continued. Augustus had another lake dug on the other side of the Tiber, somewhere in the Jewish district, now called Trastevere, and in 2 BC he organised an impressive sea battle to mark the dedication of a Temple to Mars Ultor (the avenging Mars). Its theme was the famous naval battle of Salamis in 480 BC, in which the Greeks defeated the Persians. On an artificial lake of some 540 by 350 metres with an island in the centre, just like the Bay of Salamis, thirty biremes and triremes and dozens of small craft engaged each other. As well as the oarsmen, a number not mentioned in the sources, 3,000 troops were on board the ships.[144]

The biggest sea battle ever staged took place in AD 52, during the reign of Emperor Claudius. Nineteen thousand oarsmen and soldiers fought on triremes and quadriremes, representing a 'Rhodian' and a 'Sicilian' fleet. According to Tacitus,[145] there was sufficient space on Lake Fucino for the warships to carry out full war manoeuvres. To prevent crew members from trying to escape, the entire battle scene was surrounded by floating rafts and ships full of soldiers who watched the proceedings closely. Before the battle started, the participants, condemned prisoners of war and slaves, are said to have greeted Claudius with the words that have often been attributed to all gladiators (see page 163): *'Ave Caesar, morituri te salutant'* (Hail, Caesar, those who are about to die salute you).[146] Claudius is said to have shouted back *'Aut non'* (or not), whereupon the combatants decided to forgo the battle, thinking he had set them free. But that was not what Claudius meant. He could not decide whether to have them killed by the sword or by fire. In the end he jumped out of his seat and ran along the edge of the lake, only for his hobbling gait to make all those watching him laugh. By issuing threats and holding out the prospect of future rewards, he managed to persuade them to fight after all. This is how Tacitus describes what happened:

> Although both sides were composed of criminals, nevertheless they fought with truly heroic courage and after a great many had fallen, they were spared complete annihilation.[147]

All the sea battles mentioned up to this point were held on specially created lakes, not in existing arenas. But some emperors, in their pursuit of absolute power, wanted to adapt the Circus Maximus and the Colosseum so they could serve as settings for their fantasies, as a symbolic way of displaying their power over the sea. It was not enough for them that the arena already featured tricks performed by trained crocodiles and hippopotamuses as well as land animals. They hoped that including sea battles in the programme would make an even greater impression on the public. Caligula was probably the first to attempt something like this in Rome. On the Saepta Julia, which was the venue for the gladiator shows in his day, he had a pool dug with space for just one ship. It brought him nothing but ridicule.[148] Nero had his wooden theatre filled with water, then stocked it with fish and large aquatic animals and gave the starting signal for a sea battle between the Athenians and the Persians. When the battle was over he let the water out again. Before the ground had time to dry, gladiators were sent on, not just pairs engaged in single combat, but whole groups of them at once.[149]

Titus was the third emperor to organise a sea battle in a Roman arena. He chose to re-enact the battle between

A seventeenth-century engraving showing an entirely
imaginary *naumachia* in an amphitheatre

the people of Corcyra and the Corinthians at the
beginning of the Peloponnesian War (431–404 BC). It is
the only sea battle in an arena that we can say much
about, not because ancient authors give us a great deal
of information, but because the Colosseum arena had a
surface area of only 80 by 54 metres, which set definite
limits to the battle. There are only two possibilities:
either there were two life-sized warships – most likely
triremes – simply sitting on the water while soldiers on
deck fought each other, or smaller ships sailed around
performing famous nautical manoeuvres from the
annals of maritime history.

Titus probably saw this sea battle in the Colosseum as
a one-off event. He organised a proper *naumachia* (in
this case a confrontation between Athenians and men
from Syracuse, based on the battle for Sicily in 414 BC) at

another location, a lake that Augustus had dug on the banks of the Tiber.[150] Martial is full of admiration:

> Augustus once had large numbers of ships fight here
> to the loud blaring of ships' trumpets.
> What is that worth compared to Caesar's[151] games?
>   The sea goddesses
> descried creatures here that they had never seen
>   before
> and Triton saw wagons charge into the mists of the
>   sea
> and thought of his master's horses.
> And Nereus wanted to engage ships in furious battle
> but had trouble with aquatic stage fright!
> Every kind of entertainment the circus and the
>   theatre have to offer
> is staged here on Caesar's rich waves.
> Not another word about Fucinus and Nero's lake,
> this is the *naumachia* that deserves to be
>   immortalised.[152]

Titus' brother Domitian, who succeeded him a year after the games that marked its opening, made the Colosseum permanently unsuitable for the *naumachia*, but only after he had held one more sea battle, probably to forestall any criticism that he was not capable of achieving what his brother had done. He then converted the empty space under the Colosseum into a so-called *hypogeum*. Two levels of cells and pens were built for the gladiators and for the wild animals, separated by walls and passageways. This made it impossible ever to fill the arena with water again.

Sea battles did continue, Domitian himself organised

several, but at locations with more space for 'real' naval engagements. Domitian had the choice of a number of sites that had already been used for this form of combat. For a battle scene he could have chosen the lake dug by Augustus, as his brother had, or Claudius' lake. But wilful as he was he chose a new location next to the Tiber and built extensive facilities for the audience around it. Here as elsewhere in Rome, sea battles would be held repeatedly, the last of them probably in AD 247 on the initiative of Emperor Philippus the Arabian. Although the sources do not mention the scale of this battle, we know from the way that he staged gladiator fights that the public entertainments he produced were always on a lavish scale.

Dead Meat[153]

After the spectators have left the Colosseum, a powerful atmosphere of death and decay lingers in the underground passageways. Carcasses of wild animals lie everywhere, along with the corpses of executed criminals, horribly mutilated by the claws and teeth of predators. Everything is drenched in blood and there remains a penetrating odour of rotting flesh. But since there may well be another show within a few days, perhaps even next day, everything has to look clean again. For the large permanent staff of the Colosseum and the extra manpower hired for the occasion, a dispiriting task now begins: clearing out all the corpses and carcasses.

Gladiator Burials

The easiest solution would have been to burn all the bodies, but that was not a feasible option. Lighting a huge pyre in the city was far too dangerous. Staff would first have to throw the bodies into a big pile, then load them on to carts and take them away to a place where they could be burned. Human flesh is not very flammable, so they would have had to add wood, tar and papyrus to the pyres for them to be at all effective. Another solution would have been to carry all the bodies away and dump them in a specific place. But this was not an option either, because the status of the victims was far too diverse. Choices had to be made about who should end up where. It was not only a matter of the authorities wanting to maintain the status of the deceased even after death; friends, colleagues or relatives of a gladiator who had died an honourable death also wanted to keep his body apart from the rest. They would insist that he be given an appropriate funeral. It was unthinkable that a gladiator who had been ceremonially carried out of the arena through the Porta Libitinaria would be buried in the same place as a victim of the lunchtime executions, who had been dragged out with a meat hook.

The most humiliating fate that could befall a gladiator after his death was to be given no funeral at all. His body would not be covered with earth which meant, so the Romans believed, that his soul could never find peace and would continue to walk abroad in the land of the living. He was denied even the most basic ritual, the scattering of three handfuls of sand over his body. He was thrown into a ravine outside the city boundary or left in a remote spot, usually not very far from one of the main highways. The authorities felt that tradition was on their side, because even in the earliest times, under the monarchy, criminals had been denied a final resting place. Such a punishment was regarded as entirely just in the case of murderers, because they had forfeited their rights and their place in society, so they could no longer lay any claim to peace after death.

Many of the victims of the midday executions were taken to the Tiber and cast into the river from bridges or quaysides. This was actually an even more humiliating fate than being dumped at a remote place, because it happened as the people of Rome stood and watched. This punishment had been applied throughout recorded history to people who had murdered their own relatives. The Romans believed it had a purifying effect, since scores would finally be settled with the person in question and at the same time everything that could possibly remind people of him would be swept away. Even emperors, if they had gone too far in the eyes of the people and had come to be regarded as murderers themselves, risked being thrown into the river when they died. Vitellius, who was emperor for three months in AD 69, quickly made people want to wash their hands of him and suffered as a result. He was slowly tortured to death and then dragged into the Tiber with a meat hook. When Commodus the emperor-gladiator died on the last day of AD 192, he only escaped ending up in the Tiber because his successor Pertinax intervened. In AD 222, Heliogabalus was less fortunate. After he had been killed in a lavatory, his body was carried in triumph through the city and horribly mutilated, then weighed down with stones and thrown from a bridge into the Tiber.

The victims of the Colosseum who were denied funerals included many Christians. Their refusal to participate in the emperor cult made them outcasts who might easily be accused of extremely serious crimes and forced to undergo terrible torments. Because the Romans were fully aware of the significance for Christians of the burial and subsequent resurrection of the body, they did all they could to quash any expectation of being raised again. The agonies of the arena were followed by mutilations after death, intended to destroy the integrity and purity of the body that were so important to Christians for their day of resurrection. The process was ghastly but effective. The bodies were thrown to the dogs, the remains divided up and the body parts dumped at remote places or thrown into the Tiber. Some body parts were buried, while others were burned and the ashes strewn at various different locations.

Some of the people condemned to death did not even make it as far as the ravine or the Tiber. Their torture, death and 'burial' all took place inside the pens where wild animals were held. We have good evidence that Caligula ordered condemned men to be thrown to wild animals as food and even watched his orders being carried out,[154] but it would hardly be surprising to find that more reputable emperors too, confronted by a shortage of animal feed, sometimes resorted to such measures.

As for gladiators who succumbed to their wounds or were given the *coup de grâce* at the behest of the emperor and people, they would have done well to have saved up enough to pay for a tomb. Otherwise the chances were that they would end up nameless in a mass grave. It seems probable that most of the gravestones still extant today were for gladiators who had joined a *collegium*, a kind of gladiators' trade union. One of the purposes of such a union was to use financial contributions from members to secure a final resting place for each of them. This might be a simple grave with a gravestone on which his most important feats of arms were recorded, or a niche in a communal burial chamber where the urn containing his ashes was interred. The advantage of the communal chamber was that relatives of members of the same union could mourn together and honour the memory of the deceased collectively.

A few gladiators were given high-profile funerals, reflecting the fame they had enjoyed in life. But these must have been high-ranking gladiators who had earned a lot of money for themselves and their managers. Their next-of-kin adopted the funeral rites of the Roman elite. The body was rubbed with ointment and laid for several days on a bier, adorned with flowers and wreaths. Then it was cremated and the ashes ceremonially interred in a grave, which the successful gladiator had bought while he was still alive.

Carcasses: Disposed of or Eaten?

The gladiator games involved the slaughter of thousands of animals. The greater the number of animals used, the greater the problem of disposing of the carcasses after-wards. Animals of up to about 90 kilos could be thrown on to carts and driven away just like human corpses. Carcasses of lions and tigers weighing several hundred kilos were harder to move, not to mention the vast weight of even one hippopotamus, rhinoceros or elephant. Nevertheless, a large proportion of the carcasses went the same way as the bodies of men killed in the arena. They ended up in deep ravines, remote places, or specially dug pits. The trained predators, who performed their tricks repeatedly, needed feeding. Along with the flesh of smaller animals, fed to them live, the predators were given the remains of deer, antelope and other animals killed during hunting events in the arena. This kept costs down. When an emperor held a show lasting several days, spectacular predators might have to appear in the arena a second time after a successful fight, so extra supplies of meat were always welcome.

In spite of all this forward planning, dead animals must really have started to mount up during shows lasting more than a week. It took so much time to take away all the carcasses that many were left lying around, with all the obvious dangers of decomposition, maggots, insects and infectious disease. The organisers must have seized on any means of reducing the pile. Human consumption of meat from the dead animals was one solution. Prominent Romans were not among the potential consumers, since they had enough money to eat a varied or even quite extravagant diet every day. They liked to consult a cookery book written by Apicius, a collection of carefully composed recipes from the first century, which instructed readers on how to prepare whole ostriches, ducks, geese, turtle doves, peacocks and pheasants, and the flesh of deer, boar, pigs, sheep, goats, hares and rabbits in a variety of ways. It would have been beneath them to try to get hold of meat from the arena. It seems almost as unlikely that artisans and self-employed people would commonly have queued up for pieces of meat. For them it was not so much a matter of status as the fact that they had enough money to buy meat fairly regularly. Excavations at the foot of the Palatine Hill have revealed an ancient rubbish heap with large deposits of pig, goat, chicken and duck bones. This supports the assumption that in the nearby districts where a lot of artisans lived, meat was eaten regularly.

The great mass of poor Romans lived in different conditions altogether. They were intermittently employed, if at all, and had barely enough to live on. They depended on contributions from the authorities for anything to supplement their basic diet. Emperors and prominent senators were conscious that people were dependent on them and they responded cleverly, not because they felt socially engaged and responsible for the fluctuating fortunes of the people, but because it was hard to gauge the political risk posed by a discontented populace. They did all they could to optimise the supply of grain and to avoid shortages. The very poorest citizens could claim a monthly allowance of a little over 30 kilograms of grain for themselves and their families. The rest could buy grain on the open market at reduced prices. But this only added up to very basic support. Other food products, such as olive oil and wine, were provided only very occasionally. The diet of most ordinary people could be described as meagre, poor in both calories and protein. Their daily diet consisted of bread and barley porridge enriched with olive oil, *garum* (a fish sauce used as a flavouring) and occasionally some vegetables or fruit.

It is easy to imagine how gratefully the plebs would have accepted any addition to this meagre diet, especially meat. Large numbers of people must have applied. Of course they preferred eating smaller animals such as hares, rabbits and pheasants, but meat from large wild animals must have been welcome too. All these animals had been killed fighting or in hunting events rather than by disease, so they were fit for human consumption. The Roman plebs would probably have taken the same attitude as the people in Apuleius' *Metamorphoses*.[155] In a Greek city, a magistrate assembled people and animals for a gladiator show that was to include a large number of bears. The animals arrived several days before the spectacle began, but because of the extreme heat many died before the games started. Their carcasses were left lying in the streets. Not for long, though. People turned up and, being so poverty-stricken, started to fill their stomachs with the flesh of the dead bears. Presumably Apuleius means that they cut the bears open, took the meat away with them and prepared it at home.

The decision of the organisers to share out the meat from the arena among needy citizens should be seen in this context. Everyone benefited, both the ordinary people, who got a little extra food, and the emperor in whose name the games were being held. By giving people the kind of food they seldom if ever consumed, he was able to demonstrate one more time, right at the end of the games, that he was their benefactor. The people appreciated this and praised him, forgetting for a while to ask themselves whether or not he was a good emperor. This is demonstrated by the fact that the death of the insane Caligula was greeted with such public sorrow. Flavius Josephus writes:

> For their part, the womenfolk and young people reacted the way the stupid masses always react. They had been won over by his theatre shows and his gladiator games and occasional handouts of meat.[156]

Caligula was a fanatical fan of the gladiator shows, so it is quite possible that the handouts of meat mentioned here took place immediately after the games. Tertullian makes a direct connection between the killing of wild animals and the eating of meat. In response to the Roman accusation that the Christians were cannibals, he hits back with the observation that the Romans should be called cannibals themselves, because they eat the meat of wild animals from the arena (deer, wild boar and bears).[157]

If the Romans did indeed eat the meat of animals killed in the arena, the next question is, how did they organise the distribution of the meat? Sharing it out on a 'first come, first served' basis would have caused tremendous chaos. The organisers must have come up with a system that avoided riots and disorder. It must also have been essential to prevent the strongest and cleverest people from getting to the front of the queue every time. The only way to achieve all this would have been to link the distribution of meat to attendance at the gladiator shows, by selecting the beneficiaries from among the crowd that attended the games. This would have made for a relatively simple system. We have seen that at the end of every show lottery tokens were thrown into the arena, each with the name of an article that could be picked up later. The lucky winner could exchange his lottery ball for a vase, a jug, or an item of food after the show. Along with wine, olive oil, fish sauce and grain, some meat from the arena or skins of dead animals may have found their way to the public by this route. Hares, rabbits and pheasants could no doubt be collected immediately after the performances finished, but people must have had to wait longer for pieces of meat from a deer, wild boar, bear or lion, probably until the following day when the butchers had hacked the wild animals open, boned and jointed them. The fortunate spectator would receive his prize on handing over his lottery token.

The sight of proletarian Romans hurrying home, bending under the weight of great chunks of dripping meat, must sometimes have been a prominent feature of the street scene near the Colosseum. It probably attracted little attention in a city where standards of hygiene were abominable, where both human and animal excrement was left lying in the streets, where flies, dogs and vultures were ubiquitous and where sheep and cows were daily led along the roads to the city abattoirs or slaughtered in the street.

The End of Gladiator Shows

For the first two centuries AD the Romans revelled in the gladiator games and they were a part of everyday life. Even in the third century, when the economy went into serious decline and sponsors had great difficulty finding enough money to put on spectacular shows, the violence of the arena continued to attract its fans. Gladiatorial combat still spoke to the imagination – it symbolised the grandeur of Roman supremacy. Its traditional Roman virtues, of bravery, strength and daring had an enduring appeal to the public. Against this background it seems very unlikely that any serious measures were set in train to abolish gladiator fights. After all, that would have meant not only an outright ban on a highly successful form of popular entertainment, but also a complete change to the existing rules and to the pattern of norms and values on which the gladiator games were founded. In any case, the emperor and the games were closely bound up together. Holding shows in the Colosseum gave the emperor the opportunity to prove how powerful he was, time after time, and this was seen, acknowledged and appreciated by visitors from every stratum of society. So any protest against the games was a protest against the power of the emperor. Anyone taking such an initiative would have had to challenge him openly and question his authority. Critics of the gladiator shows were not willing to go that far.

Objections to Gladiator Fights

There were people though, who, without calling for an outright ban, did voice their objections to the gore of the arena. If we set out to look for critics with ethical objections we quickly arrive at Cicero and Seneca. They were figureheads of an intellectual elite who wanted nothing to do with the amphitheatre and made no secret of the repugnance they felt for such bloodthirsty violence. But if we look more closely at what these two authors actually said about the different elements that made up the gladiator shows, their disgust seems remarkably mild. Though they are critical of the fights, they cannot hide their admiration for the bravery and courage of the main players, despite the fact that such men have virtually lost the right to a life worthy of a human being. If complete outcasts can prove they have moral backbone, then everyone must have it in them. Cicero articulates this way of thinking very clearly in *The Tusculum Disputations*. Having explained that the arena is the place where courage is most clearly demonstrated (see page 40), he discusses the way it relates to 'normal' society:

> Is it possible that a filthy Samnite, who deserves his life and his station, could be capable of this [that is, the manifestation of virtue], while a man who was born for fame has a place deep within him that is so weak it cannot be hardened by exercise or theoretical study? Some people think that gladiator shows are cruel and inhumane and perhaps in their present form they are. When criminals fought to the death, sword in hand, there may have been more effective ways to accustom our ears to pain and death, but not so our eyes.[158]

Cicero believes the gladiator shows have an educational value to the extent that the courage shown in the arena sets an example to be followed. People at the very lowest levels of society hold up a mirror, as it were, to the rest. But that was as far as the positive side went. Everything else that Cicero writes makes it clear he was critical of the whole business of gladiator shows. In 55 BC, when Pompey was about to hold a very expensive show, Cicero wrote in a letter to a friend[159] that he cannot understand how any right-thinking, well-educated person could possibly enjoy the games. He asks himself how anyone could feel enthusiasm for shows in which animals are chased around the arena for five days in a row, in which a defenceless human being is ripped apart by wild animals or a beautiful creature speared by a huntsman. He writes that Pompey himself admitted that in fact it was all a waste of time and money. Putting on such a show was no more than a cheap triumph that would quickly evaporate. But Cicero must have had some degree of understanding for Pompey's position, because in a piece he wrote in defence of Sestius in 57 BC, he says that there are three situations in which it is possible to quantify public opinion and desire: public meetings and elections, and after fights in the arena.[160] He goes on to explain how the crowd acts as a political barometer during gladiator fights, welcoming one politician with cheers and greeting another with catcalls.

Seneca shared Cicero's reservations about gladiator shows. Like Cicero, he admired the gladiators' virtues, given that they were men at the bottom of the social pile, but he also expresses his disapproval of everything that accompanied these events. He targets the crowd in particular, the irrational, unquestioning masses who turned up without fail to see every spectacle. Seneca believes that intellectuals should keep right away from the arena, leaving it to ordinary people to be endlessly amused by limitless slaughter. It was particularly important for intellectuals to avoid those parts of the programme that arouse our most primitive desires. Seneca makes it clear what he means by this in a letter. He is referring to the lunchtime executions. These involve acts that go against even the most basic ethical standards:

What do I think you should avoid in particular? The crowd! You are not yet capable of entrusting yourself to it with any confidence. At least, I must confess my own weakness: I never return home the same person. Something I'd managed to pacify is disturbed, something I'd driven out comes back.

By chance I was at a lunchtime performance recently, expecting to find some amusement, humour and relaxation – at that time of day one generally sees something other than bloodletting. But that's not how things turned out. It seems to me now that people were better off with the way the fights used to be held; nowadays the more trivial events have been dispensed with and the fights are sheer slaughter. The fighters have nothing to protect themselves with, they stand there with their entire bodies exposed to whatever is thrown at them and they never make a move without hitting their target. Spectators usually find this more fun than ordinary duels or request acts. It really is more 'fun' too: no helmet, no shield to deflect sword thrusts! Armour? Martial arts? Things like that only get in death's way! In the mornings people are thrown to the lions and bears. In the afternoons they are thrown to the crowd, and the crowd demands that murderers come face to face with the people who will kill them in their turn, and they save the winner for a subsequent slaughter. For the combatants the proceedings always end in death and everything is decided by fire and sword. And so it goes on, to fill the time in the arena.

'But that chap has committed robbery with violence, he's killed a man!'

So what? As a murderer he is receiving the punishment he deserves, but you, poor spectator, what have you done to deserve having to watch?

'Finish him off! Thrash him to shreds! Into the flames with him! Why so careful with that sword? That thrust lacked conviction! How unsporting, not wanting to die! Thrash them, then they'll have to fight! Make them lay into each other without any clothes on, that always gets results!'

Then the intermission begins. 'Let's carry out a few executions while we're waiting. Otherwise there's nothing to do!'[161]

Seneca is only describing the lunchtime executions here. He makes no comment on the gladiator fights, indeed he barely mentions them in any of his writings. He does not criticise the shows directly, but limits himself to remarks that are mainly included for their entertainment value. Because of the veiled nature of his criticism, it is difficult to determine whether he was fundamentally opposed to the games. We can certainly assume he was less than an enthusiastic fan, but that does not make him a self-declared opponent, although people have often regarded him as such on the basis of his letter to Lucilius quoted above. Seneca's view was no exception in the first century AD. He was supported by other authors of his time who had little liking for the gladiator games, which were after all intended to play upon the most primitive emotions of the crowd. But they openly admired the gladiators' heroic performances.

The historian Tacitus is totally negative. A pessimist, with a sarcastic take on his own times, he believed that historians should concern themselves with issues of substance and not trivial matters like gladiator shows, so he offers no opinion at all on the subject. Only when he wants to make clear how far Rome has strayed from traditional values and the practice of the fine arts does he find himself compelled to say something about popular entertainment. His dominant feeling is one of repugnance for everyone who has anything to do with the games. He attacks senators and knights who voluntarily abase themselves by fighting as gladiators. Gladiators and criminals killed in the arena do not arouse the slightest pity in him. Gladiators are 'worthless blood' (*vilis sanguis*)[162] and it is shameful to be a descendant of one of them; they lack discipline, in short they are a bad lot. They contribute nothing in the sphere of social values and their fights only lead to the corruption of the young.

The Demise of Gladiator Shows

The costly spectacles in the Colosseum put on by Gordianus I and III and Probus might give the impression that the gladiator shows are flourishing all across the empire in the third century. The reverse is the case.

Rome is still holding on, however grimly, to its reputation as the radiant capital of an immense empire, but people in the provinces have long realised that times have changed. The western provinces are faced with invasions by barbarians and sharp economic decline, and this inevitably forces them to reconsider the use they make of their declining economic resources. In Spain, Gaul, Germany and Britain, the priests of the emperor cult and rich private citizens, who who have · always held gladiator shows fairly regularly, are now reluctant to do so. There is simply not enough money for events involving gladiators and wild animals. Local governments have to look for cheaper forms of entertainment.

In the eastern provinces the invasions do not have such a disruptive effect on the economy, but here too the number of shows declines markedly. This is mainly a result of new ways of thinking about the phenomenon after the rise and eventual dominance of Christianity, which has won many converts in the eastern empire and North Africa. To Christian ideologists the gladiator shows are beyond comprehension. Their beliefs lead them to endorse the views of Greek writers, who have already articulated their objections and who see the violent spectacles as first and foremost a threat to their own culture. The fact that an impassioned crowd can become enthusiastically caught up in a show of a type that is so alien to their own superior Greek culture is something they are simply unable to understand. This attitude is widespread among the Greek urban elites and not unknown in Rome either. Christians develop a world view that rejects (although not on the same grounds as the Greeks) any involvement with a performance so alien to them. Christian writers make their opinions very clear. Around the year AD 200 Clement of Alexandria calls the amphitheatre '*cavea saeviens*' – 'a forum that turns men into savages',[163] and Tertullian openly expresses his worries about the effect the gladiator fights have on the public.[164] At the heart of their criticism is the observation that gladiators, infamous creatures that they are, can arouse the passions of people ranked far above them. And Christians have even more reason to condemn the gladiator games categorically. In the recent past, many of their fellow believers died as martyrs in the arena, which makes it impossible for Christians to take any pleasure in this form of entertainment.

While wild animal hunts and public executions attracted far less criticism, Christians felt an abhorrence for the gladiator fights. This was partly because, in the heathen world of the Romans, the gladiator was given a chance to show his bravery in the arena and to bring about his own salvation through an amnesty from the emperor and the people. This runs completely counter to Christian teaching, which lays down that a person's salvation cannot depend on earthly powers, like the emperor and the people, but only on God who, through the sacraments, will take an individual under his protection and give him eternal life. Christian society had no need of gladiator shows as a way of symbolising the distinction between insiders and outsiders, nor as a means for outsiders to fight their way back into society.[165]

The first time gladiatorial combat was tackled head on by the authorities was in AD 325. On 1 October that year, Emperor Constantine, who for some years had felt considerable sympathy for the Christians and their institutions, produced an official document in which he addresses Maximus, governor of a region of the eastern provinces. The text of his edict is as follows:

> At a time when peace reigns everywhere and internal order has been restored, bloody shows cannot delight us. Therefore we totally forbid the existence of gladiators; see to it that persons who up until now were condemned to live as gladiators for their crimes are sent to the mines, so that they can pay for their criminal behaviour without their blood being spilt.[166]

Whether this edict issued by Constantine gave an initial impetus to the abolition of the gladiator shows is difficult to say, since its long-term effects were negligible. Perhaps it was simply a measure intended to provide more labour for the quarrying of stone, where there was a severe manpower shortage, because three years later, in AD 328, the games were held in Antioch as usual and Constantine expressed no objection. Nor did his successors object when gladiator shows were put on in other eastern cities. Bishops in those cities did decide that believers should not take on any of the practical jobs involved in putting on a show and deprived all gladiators of the right to be baptised.

In the Italian provinces there was no question of a deliberate policy of abolition. None of the Christian emperors after Constantine seems to have had any plans of that kind. In AD 333–337, Constantine's sons were still giving towns in central Italy official permission to hold gladiator shows. The famous mosaics now in the Galleria Borghese in Rome, featuring hunting scenes and gladiator fights, date from this time. They were laid in a large villa on the Via Labicana, close to the Colosseum.

Emperor Constantine

In the years that followed little or nothing seems to have changed in Rome, since Philocalus' Calendar shows ten days in AD 354 reserved for gladiator shows (see page 35). In AD 367 Valentinianus I introduced an official ban on sentencing Christians to the arena, but this punishment still applied to non-Christians.

Although no specific political steps were taken to put an end to gladiatorial combat, in the second half of the fourth century AD a gradual decline did take place in Rome. The number of people converting to Christianity grew rapidly and with every year that passed the emperors had less need to secure the people's loyalty by putting on ambitious shows. The situation in the final two decades of the fourth century must have been extremely confusing, since only contradictary and vague reports have come down to us. All that seems certain is that Emperor Theodosius I did everything in his power to ban heathen festivals. But in AD 393 Senator Symmachus put on a big gladiator show as if nothing had changed. It is possible, but unproven, that Theodosius' son and successor, Honorius, introduced a ban on gladiator schools in AD 399, thereby indirectly lowering the quality of the main players.

But Honorius did not decide to do away with the gladiator fights for good, as some people claim. The ban is said to have been introduced in AD 404 after one very unusual event. A monk called Telemachus had come to Rome from Asia Minor specifically to protest against gladiator fights. During a performance, he rushed from his seat into the arena and tried to prevent two gladiators from fighting one another. The spectators were furious. They grabbed the monk and tore him to pieces. Honorius refused to stomach this reaction and banned gladiators from Rome for good. This is little more than an anecdote, written down to underline the Christians' aversion for gladiator shows. Honorius' decision was probably only a temporary measure designed as a punishment, and even then it only applied to Rome. Over the next few years various sources report gladiator shows continuing as normal elsewhere.

It seems probable that the gladiator shows were never officially abolished but gradually died out. Theodosius had made Christianity the state religion in AD 393, which countless Christians interpreted as meaning that harsh measures against heathens now had official sanction. The Colosseum and the gladiator shows became a popular target for these measures, as symbols of defeated heathenism. Theodosius and Honorius did not need to introduce a strict ban on gladiatorial combat. Their Christian subjects took the initiative by ensuring that the supply of keen spectators declined of its own accord. Eventually there were only a few people left who felt the need to see with their own eyes how an inferior man, a gladiator, could hold up a mirror to Roman society by demonstrating his bravery. In any case, the worsening economic situation made it extremely difficult for anyone to employ enough gladiators. People who were still tempted to visit gladiator shows were not particularly thrilled by the limited programme of events on offer.

We do not know when the last fight took place, but it must have been before AD 440, because that was the year Bishop Salvianus began a sustained attack on public shows in general and wild animal chases, theatrical events and chariot races in particular. Gladiator fights are not mentioned in his pamphlet, which can only mean that they had already disappeared or been marginalised. The killing of wild animals still went on. It seems Christians believed violence against animals was something of a quite different order, as were fights between people and animals, which also continued as before. As ever, Rome was no exception in this, even though the city had been plundered a number of times in the fifth century and hit by several earthquakes, which had prompted many people to leave. The city's population declined dramatically, further reducing the number of potential spectators. One of the last occasions when animals appeared in the arena in Rome was in AD 519. The Gothic King Theoderik, who wanted nothing to do with popular entertainment in the Colosseum, had given his son-in-law Cilica permission to celebrate his recent appointment as consul by putting on an appropriate show. The account provided by Cassiodorus, Lord Chamberlain to Theoderik, in which he explicitly mentions that the spectators watched the African wild animals in wonder and amazement,[167] suggests that by this point they must have been deprived of shows like this for quite some time.

Meanwhile Constantinople had taken on the role played until then by Rome, not only as a centre of political power but as the main place where Roman popular entertainment was available in all its many guises. Along with the immensely popular chariot races, wild animal hunts and fights between men and animals also remained on the programme, although more and more people in the new Rome were starting to ask themselves what made these events so special. Their obsolescence came only very gradually. Fights between men and animals were banned at the start of the sixth century, but hunting shows continued as before. Emperor Justinian organised a big hunting event as late as AD 536. After that, even this feature of the Roman gladiator games seems to have disappeared.

The Decline and Fall of the Colosseum

As long as the Colosseum remains, Rome will remain,
When the Colosseum falls, Rome will fall.
And the fall of Rome means the fall of the whole
world.[168]

The Venerable Bede

As the fifth century progressed, Rome finally lost the brilliance of the eternal city. Rome had long since been reliant on its provinces, living off their tax payments. But in some provinces economic decline had such a forceful impact that it became impossible to collect taxes, whether in cash or in kind, and naturally this had repercussions for Rome. It was impossible to live off the profits from the landed estates in the surrounding countryside, because the land had fallen into neglect. The people of Rome, accustomed to 'bread and circuses', would now have to support themselves. A large proportion of them, proving incapable of this, died of hunger, or of the malaria that spread through the landed estates as they deteriorated into marshland and subsequently took its toll on Rome. Large groups of people who had survived the disease left the city and settled in smaller agricultural towns in the hills of central Italy. The decline in population in the fifth century must have been quite dramatic. In the years around AD 400, Rome still had approximately 800,000 inhabitants, by the middle of the fifth century this had dropped to 500,000 and by 500 there were only 100,000 left. Around 568, under threat from the Langobardi, the population reached a low of 30,000. By the end of the sixth century this number had increased again to around 90,000, but in the centuries that followed it was never to rise much above 100,000 and often fell far below that.

By the fifth and sixth centuries, a few historic buildings were all that was left to remind people of the grandeur of first- and second-century imperial Rome. These buildings had not been destroyed by the Goths and Vandals who took Rome in 410 and 455, but they had certainly been plundered. Cassiodorus paints a dispiriting picture of the Rome of his day. He writes of collapsed grain silos, bronze statues pulled from their pedestals and marble pillars sawn into pieces for use elsewhere. What Cassiodorus describes was only the beginning of the demolition of the great classical buildings. A thousand years later, at the end of the Middle Ages, the situation was far worse. In fact by then whole areas had been cleared. Anyone looking for building materials knew he had a good chance of finding something suitable at the Roman Forum or in the Colosséum. The popes, who wanted to give Rome the gloss of Christianity, certainly played an important role in this destruction. Ancient Roman architecture had to be cleared to make way for new churches and palaces.

After the gladiator shows ended, the Colosseum quickly became an empty and desolate pile of rock. No maintenance was carried out and its decay was accelerated by natural disasters. A number of powerful earthquakes in the Middle Ages had devastating effects.

The earthquake of 508 alone must have caused extensive damage. Part of the colonnade around the highest galleries collapsed. Chunks of falling masonry transformed the lower rows of seating into heaps of rubble. To reduce the danger of further collapse, a huge amount of rubble was removed and dumped in the space under the arena. The sewage system had broken down, so the substructure, the *hypogeum*, where the wild animals and the gladiators had once waited in their pens and cells before being sent up into the light, was repeatedly flooded and became overgrown with weeds.

In the sixth century, by which time there were no longer any performances in the Colosseum, the entrances were blocked. But most people ignored the ban on entering the building. Plunderers great and small went about their business unimpeded. Herdsmen adapted the spaces under the seating to serve as animal stalls. There they were joined by the Roman underclass: beggars, tramps and street robbers slept in the passageways or under the arches of the outer wall. In due course blacksmiths, coppersmiths, shoe-cleaners, bricklayers, carpenters, lime burners and peddlers moved in to set up workshops and to sell their wares.

By the Middle Ages, many myths and legends had grown up around the Colosseum. The *Mirabilia urbis Romae*, a travel guide for pilgrims dating from the early eleventh century, describes the Colosseum as a heathen temple to the Sun, completely roofed over with a dome of golden bronze. A statue of Apollo was said to have stood in the middle, holding a globe in one hand to symbolise Rome's power over the whole world. In subsequent centuries the 'temple' was no longer seen as having been connected exclusively with the Sun but with all the gods, which made it a kind of second Pantheon. Many people believed the legend that claimed the poet Virgil had designed the Colosseum and later studied magic there. Even as late as the sixteenth century, when a great deal more was known about the true meaning and function of the Colosseum in the ancient world, tales of black magic still lingered. The sculptor and writer Benvenuto Cellini is said to have brought the forces of evil that had established themselves in the Colosseum under control, on the advice of a priest from Sicily. One night he entered the old arena along with a priest and a young man. He drew lines on the ground and designated the area inside them a magic space. Cellini himself claims the session was a success. He sprinkled fragrant perfumes and lit flaming torches, and the forces of the devil were compelled to move out.[169]

An impression of the Colosseum with the huge statue of Apollo in the middle, painted by the sixteenth-century artist Maarten van Heemskerck

But by the time Cellini was able to visit the Colosseum at will, a great deal had changed. Shortly after 1084, everyone living in the Colosseum was evicted. Led by Robert Guiscard, the Normans plundered Rome and partly destroyed it. Aristocratic families went looking for fortified places where they would feel safe. The Savelli family occupied Marcellus' Theatre, the Colonna family took possession of Augustus' Mausoleum and the Frangipani family moved into the Colosseum and the surrounding area. They managed to remain resident there for more than two centuries, until 1312. Then they in turn were forced to relinquish the Colosseum.

On 1 September 1332, not many years after the Frangipani family had left, a remarkable spectacle took place in the Colosseum: bullfights to mark the visit of King Louis of Bavaria. They were very much like the ancient animal fights, although neither the organisers nor the appreciative audience were aware of this. Men entered the arena armed only with meat skewers. According to one account by Ludovico Bonconte Monaldeschi, eleven bulls died that day and eighteen bullfighters. The dead were given a solemn funeral in the churches of Santa Maria Maggiore and San Giovanni in Laterano. Although various proposals were put forward, the performance was never repeated.[170]

In 1349, Rome was again hit by an earthquake. The damage to the Colosseum was not great, but because the quake wreaked havoc in the surrounding area and a number of nearby churches were abandoned, the amphitheatre was left isolated, a huge stone shell in an abandoned district. The beggars, peddlers and magicians returned, followed in the fifteenth century by the pope's own city planners, more fanatical than ever in their

212

determination to wipe out any trace of pagan Rome. It almost seemed as if every new pope wanted to outdo his predecessor by coming up with even more ambitious building plans, and ancient classical monuments suffered as a result. A large amount of marble and stone from the Colosseum went into building the Palazzo Venezia, the Palazzo Farnese, the Palazzo della Cancellaria and St Peter's. Every year, thousands of tons of building material must have been loaded on to wagons and moved to the new building sites. One bill written out in 1452, under Pope Nicholas V, gives us an idea of the extent of the transport operation involved. Between September 1451 and May 1452, 2,522 tons of marble and stone were removed from the Colosseum. Not long afterwards there were signs that the popes might now leave the remaining ruins alone, since in 1462 Pius II, one of the few popes with extensive knowledge of the classics, introduced a law placing several historic buildings including the Colosseum on a list of protected monuments. But his successors had other ideas. They reverted to the earlier building policy and set about developing Christian Rome further, at the expense of its pagan monuments. People gradually forgot about the Colosseum of the gladiators. The real heroes were now the martyrs who had given their blood for Christ and prepared the way for the rise of Christian Rome.

Papal propaganda for the Christian Colosseum was disseminated widely. More and more believers made a pilgrimage to Rome to visit the places where Ignatius and all his fellow martyrs had lost their lives. In 1749, Benedict XIV officially consecrated the already established Stations of the Cross and the arena became an official memorial to the martyrs. Pilgrims kissed the

Capriccio with Colosseum, a painting by the eighteenth-
century artist B. Bellotto

large cross in the middle of the arena for an indulgence
of 100 days and walked past the Stations of the Cross
near the lowest rows of seating, or climbed to the top to
plant crosses there. One hermit had withdrawn to a
space under the old galleries as if he wanted to protect
the holiness of the place. And between all the Christian

places of remembrance, herdsmen shuffled to and fro with their sheep and goats.

In the eighteenth and nineteenth centuries, travellers with an artistic bent started to arrive on the Grand Tour. Whether they reacted with delight or with dismay on finding the classical Colosseum buried under a layer of Christian propaganda, the experience as a whole always made an overwhelming and indelible impression on them. They wrote about it in prose or verse, or recorded their impressions in paintings. The moonlit arena sometimes inspired them to set a passage of a novel or story in the Colosseum, although this often involved no more than a simple background detail, such as the screechings of the owl in Lord Byron's drama *Manfred*, or, much later, the romance at the foot of the great cross in the middle of the arena in Henry James' novella *Daisy Miller*. These passages do nevertheless give us an impression of the atmosphere in the Colosseum as experienced by visitors.[171] Sometimes a writer allows us to share his more profound thoughts. One very telling description can be found in the personal reflections on the transience of things in a letter to a friend written by French romantic writer Chateaubriand in 1804:

One beautiful evening this past month of July, I went into the Colosseum and sat on the steps of one of the altars dedicated to the Stations of the Cross. The setting sun poured gold down over all the galleries, where a flood of people once poured through; at the same time deep shadows emerged from the recesses of the upper galleries and walkways, and broad strips of black shadow fell upon the ground. Standing on the thick walls I could see beyond the ruins, to the right of the building, the garden of the palace of the emperors with a palm tree, as if planted deliberately on the ruins as a tribute to artists and poets. Instead of cries of joy from the savage spectators of times gone by as they watched Christians being ripped apart by lions and panthers, I could hear only the barking of the dogs belonging to the hermits who guard these ruins. But when the sun goes down below the horizon, the clock of St Peter's echoes through the vaulted arcades of the Colosseum. That unanimity, produced by the religious sounds that can be heard between the two greatest monuments of heathen and Christian Rome, touched me deeply; I contemplated the fact that, just like this ancient edifice, the great modern building will crumble in its turn and monuments succeed each other like the people who establish them; I remembered that the very same Jews who worked on the great buildings of Egypt and Babylonia during their first period of captivity had built this enormous circular wall during their last diaspora and that the monument whose vaults echoed to the sound of the Christian clock was the work of a heathen emperor, said in the prophecies to be preordained to become the man who would raze Jerusalem to the ground. My dear friend, are these not elevated topics to consider, brought to our attention by this one ruin? And do you not think that a city where such stimulating thoughts are to be encountered at every step must be worth visiting?[172]

The far off times of the heathen Colosseum were, quite unintentionally, brought to life in a rather remarkable way by the botanist Richard Deakin. He was one of the last people to study the Colosseum in its natural state. He searched all the cracks and crannies of the arena, the galleries and passageways, looking for both flowering and non-flowering plants. Within its walls he discovered no less than 420 botanical species. Deakin claims that the seeds of some rare plants were transported from distant lands in the fur of wild animals, to grow and bloom here. Deakin must have been a very devout man, since he makes a direct connection between the crown of thorns and the 'eternal crown without thorns' that was conferred on martyrs in the arena. In 1855 he described his botanical quest in a book, *Flora in the Colosseum*.

Nineteen years later, in 1874, the Colosseum was handed over to the archaeologists. This brought an end to church control. The cross in the middle of the arena, the Stations of the Cross, the trees and plants and the hermits were all cleared to make way for the work of the archaeologists. And although the clergy made a great deal of fuss and protest marches were held in and around the amphitheatre, the new holders of power, who wanted to establish a connection between themselves and the history of ancient Rome, were not to be dissuaded. They removed the sections of wall that had been shaken loose by earthquakes and had crashed down into the underground vaults of the arena, and they were then able to see the original shape of the walls, cells and pens. This made clear for the first time just how ingenious the system had been that allowed wild animals to be brought up into the arena effortlessly, using hoists.

The excavation work was given fresh impetus in the 1930s. Mussolini, *il Duce*, regarded the ancient

Colosseum as irrefutable proof of the power of the Roman emperors and he wanted to make this monument to Rome's great and glorious past accessible to the public. Archaeologists were ready to co-operate in achieving this, but in their haste to expose the ancient building work they made a number of significant errors. They built steps up through the lowest rows of seating, where the senators' thrones had stood.This did not worry Mussolini and his followers, as long as the Colosseum was made to look like a majestic monument that would call forth memories of illustrious emperors.Whole residential districts were flattened to provide a better view of Marcellus' Theatre, the Roman Forum and the Colosseum.Thousands of houses standing in the way of a direct route from the Colosseum to the Campidoglio and the Palazzo Venezia, his official headquarters, were demolished and a broad new thoroughfare was built, the Via del Impero – its name was changed to the Via dei Fori Imperiali after the Second World War – linking ancient Rome to the new Rome.

In 1938, Mussolini played host to Hitler.As the Führer rode from the Central Station to the Campidoglio, the ancient monuments were lit by 45,000 lamps hanging from a total of 160 kilometres of cable. Unfortunately for Hitler, it rained so heavily while he was in Rome that some parts of the programme, including several military parades, had to be cancelled.This did give him a chance to spend more time than originally planned in the Colosseum during the several days he spent in the city. Red lights were set up everywhere for the occasion, giving the Colosseum an unreal, almost blood-soaked appearance. To Hitler the place recalled the dynamism of the powerful emperors who had managed to construct such a building and then made every possible effort to display their power by putting on shows that were truly stunning. Was it not the case that the Colosseum was built by slaves from conquered regions? Had they not mainly been Jewish prisoners of war, captured when Jerusalem was taken in AD 70? And had this not made the Colosseum an everlasting symbol of the power of the Roman emperors? Hitler wanted to emulate them, which meant copying their building policies. He got archaeologists to tell him about the Colosseum's design and construction, and he conceived a plan to build a huge edifice like it in Nuremberg as a new seat for the Reichstag. In the new building, stone and marble would be used in place of iron and steel, indestructible materials that would keep his memory alive 'for eternity'. Detailed plans were worked out on paper, although fortunately the building was never constructed.[173]

Gladiator Films

At the end of the nineteenth century, when the very first films were being shown, scriptwriters and film directors turned their attention to the ancient world in an effort to find new subject matter. People at the time had become extremely interested in Greek and Roman civilisations. Texts by classical authors were being rescued from obscurity and new translations made them accessible to the layman. The physical remains of classical cultures were being unearthed at a great rate. Filmmakers watched as an ancient world emerged, suggesting innumerable themes that would fascinate the general public. It was a world of action and violence, which was a great advantage, since depictions of violent scenes on film could be quite spectacular. The violent history of the Romans had more to offer filmmakers in this respect than the history of ancient Greece and it featured a number of familiar figures who spoke to the imagination, people like Hannibal, Julius Caesar, Cleopatra, Nero and Commodus. In all, plenty to inspire the writers of scripts for gripping new films.

Three nineteenth-century historical novels were perhaps even more important as a source of inspiration for the first screenwriters than authentic sources from the ancient world. All three are set in Roman times and each takes the struggle between 'good' and 'evil' as its theme. In all three of these novels, one of the main characters is a man unjustly condemned to slavery or the death penalty who takes on evil rulers and eventually seizes the chance to avenge in the arena the injustice he has suffered outside it. The first book to extrapolate on this basic plot was *The Last Days of Pompeii*, a novel written by Lord Edward Bulwer Lytton in 1834. It is a love story about a young man called Glaucus and his sweetheart Ione, set just before the eruption of Vesuvius in AD 79. With considerable verve, the author describes the ferocious wild animals and gladiator fights in the arena. Even more popular was the novel *Fabiola* by Nicholas Wiseman, written in 1854. A story of martyrdom set in the years around AD 300 when the persecution of the Christians under Diocletian was at its height, the book was reprinted many times. But the greatest triumph of all was the novel *Quo Vadis?* by Henryk Sienkiewicz, published in 1895, for which he was awarded the Nobel Prize for Literature ten years later. Dozens of editions in a wide range of languages prove that Sienkiewicz touched a chord with many thousands of people with his retelling of the story of the persecution of the Christians under Emperor Nero and the torments inflicted on the martyrs in the arena.

The makers of the first gladiator films allowed themselves to be guided to quite a large extent by the imaginations of visual artists who had taken the phenomena of gladiatorial combat and Christian martyrdom as their subject. Paintings by Georges de la Tour (seventeenth century), Sir Lawrence Alma-Tadema (nineteenth century) and Jean-Léon Gérôme (nineteenth century) were studied in detail. Gérôme was praised more than any other painter for the way he composed his arena scenes. To many people, his *Pollice verso* of 1872 remains to this day the definitive representation of the climax of a gladiator fight. He is indeed a wonderful painter. In this painting Gérôme created a remarkable image of a victorious gladiator resting one foot on his defeated opponent, proudly looking up towards the imperial box. In the galleries the spectators, prominent among them the Vestal Virgins dressed in white, give the thumbs down as a signal that the defeated gladiator must be killed. Gérôme has even managed to lend a marvellous colour to the light, filtered through awnings stretched high over the arena.

The filming of *The Last Days of Pompeii*, *Fabiola* and *Quo Vadis?* marked the start of a long line of gladiator films, some of which turned out to be classics while others are long forgotten. Some were based on traditional stories, some on famous novels and some

Pollice verso, a painting by Jean-Léon Gérôme, 1872

sprang entirely from the imaginations of the scriptwriters. Most can now only be found in the archives of film museums. Who today remembers *Demetrius and the Gladiators*, made in 1964, or *Gladiator of Rome* of 1962? A few films did become famous. *Spartacus* and *Gladiator* in particular are films that have formed many people's impressions of the gladiator fights.

Spartacus

The rebellion led by the slave Spartacus who fled the gladiator school in Capua in 73 BC and who, with his steadily increasing following, challenged the Roman armies for almost three years (see page 30) is of course a wonderful story. Thousands of desperate slaves terrified the Romans, shaking the state to its foundations. It would have been even better from the filmmakers' point of view if justice had prevailed and the slaves had ultimately triumphed over the Roman legions. But they did not dare to introduce such a radical distortion of historical reality because it would have meant tampering with the facts handed down by Sallustius, Plutarch and Florus. We read how Spartacus, after his long wandering journey through Italy, fought bravely to the death (and was not nailed to a cross as in the film) without managing to bring about any change at all in the system of slavery.

Spartacus' uprising has been filmed five times. The best known Spartacus film was directed by Stanley Kubrick and released in 1960. It is 184 minutes long and cost $12 million to make, an astronomical sum in those days. The film brings vividly to life the whole series of confrontations between the slaves and the Roman armies, presenting them as a struggle between the humanity of the slaves and the cynical arrogance of the Roman authorities. The film is one long indictment of the inequality in law between slaves and free people, forcefully summed up in lines spoken by Spartacus himself: "A free man dies and he loses the pleasure of life; a slave loses his pain. Death is the only freedom a slave knows . . . That's why we'll win."

It is curious that Spartacus, who has gone down in history as the most famous gladiator ever, is barely given a chance to show what he can do. We see the star of the film, Kirk Douglas, in long battle scenes at the head of his army, but only once as a gladiator, just before his escape from the gladiator school in Capua. He fights as a *thraex*. This is in itself a fairly logical assumption, since Spartacus came from Thrace, but his weapons are nothing like those of a *thraex*. The very small round shield and short sword he carries bear little or no resemblance to ancient weapons and he is not wearing any kind of leg-plates or helmet.

The historian will be even more struck by the fact that Spartacus' opponent, the dark athlete Draba (played by Woody Strode) does not fight as a *gallus* or a *samnitis*, or even as a *thraex*, as would normally have been the case, but as a *retiarius*. This is admittedly quite a spectacular combination but not a historically accurate one, since the *retiarius*, whose net and trident guaranteed thrilling fights, was an invention of the later, imperial period. This type of gladiator was certainly not introduced before the reign of Augustus, more than sixty years after Spartacus' escape from Capua, and when combat involving the *retiarius* did become a regular part of the programme his opponent was never a *thraex* but always a *secutor* or a *murmillo*.

The outcome of the famous gladiator fight between Spartacus and Draba fits the pattern of the film, where 'good slaves' fight 'evil Roman politicians'. Four gladiators, Spartacus and Draba among them, are forced to put on a private show in the arena at the school in Capua for Crassus, his wife, daughter and son-in-law. There are no other spectators. At the end of a blood-curdling fight, Draba forces Spartacus to the ground with his trident. Crassus' wife gives the thumbs down to indicate that Draba must kill Spartacus, but Draba refuses. Furious, he throws his trident at Crassus. Then he climbs into the box where Crassus and his family are sitting, clearly intending to attack them. When Draba has almost reached them, one of Crassus' bodyguards throws a spear into his back. As he hangs from the edge of the box, dying, Crassus cuts his throat. Draba's body falls down into the sand on the arena floor. As far as I know, such a drama never took place in ancient times, not even under such insane emperors as Caligula, Nero, Domitian or Commodus.

Nevertheless, I regard *Spartacus* as a good film, since the historical distortions are not ultimately disturbing. The slaves Spartacus and Crixus, the Roman politicians Crassus and Caesar, the Cilician pirates and the rebellion at the gladiator school in Capua are depicted with considerable historical accuracy. After the premiere, director Stanley Kubrick himself expressed dissatisfaction with the end result. Was it false modesty or did he really mean it when he said, "I am disappointed in the film. It had everything but a good story."?[174]

Gladiator

Spartacus was produced at a time when spectacular films of its kind were popular. From the mid 1960s onwards, enthusiasm for such epics rapidly declined and violent films set in ancient Rome disappeared from cinemas. One of the last of the genre was *The Fall of the Roman Empire* of 1964, a title that suggests the story takes place in the fifth century when the fall of the Roman Empire was clearly underway. But in fact the film is all about the evil Commodus, emperor from AD 180 to 192, his tyrannical rule and his battle with a certain Livius, who eventually manages to depose him.

More than thirty years passed without a single new film about the Romans being made. It began to look as though the type of violence that had always played a major role in films about ancient Rome was gone for good. But when *Gladiator* was released in 2000, a film that made use of all the opportunities offered by computer-generated special effects, it became clear that there was still an audience for this kind of film. Perhaps it was no coincidence that director Ridley Scott chose to feature the same emperor as the makers of *The Fall of the Roman Empire*. Once again, Commodus is the malevolent main character and once again his path is crossed by a man who brings out everything that is worst in him.

There is a tightly constructed plot. The year is AD 180 and Emperor Marcus Aurelius, father of Commodus, feels he does not have long to live. He summons Maximus, general of the troops who have just emerged victorious from a fierce battle against the barbarians on the northern border, and tells him that his greatest desire is that he, Maximus, should take power after his death and make Rome a republic once again. A little later we watch as the ailing Marcus Aurelius receives Commodus. The father says what he thinks of his son and the son in turn complains that his father has never been willing to accept him for what he is. The scene ends with Commodus strangling his father and becoming the new emperor. Commodus immediately tries to kill Maximus, but Maximus manages to escape his pursuers and heads for Spain to join his wife and young son. When he arrives there he discovers that both have been killed by Commodus' soldiers. His world falls apart. The film leaps forward in time and we see Maximus, who has been captured and sold as a slave, at a gladiator school in Zucchabar in North Africa. Although at first he shows little enthusiasm for gladiatorial combat, he turns out to have a natural talent. He is more skilful than any gladiator before him. The gladiator manager Proximo takes him to Rome. In the Colosseum, Maximus turns out to be a real sensation. He displays in the arena the qualities he once displayed at the head of an army, leading his 'forces' in mass fights. His popularity grows to such an extent that he becomes caught up in plots against Commodus and is arrested. Ultimately, finding himself forced into a corner, the emperor can see no way to save himself and to neutralise Maximus other than by fighting with him man to man in a duel, but only after he has inflicted serious wounds on him in prison, wounds that later prove fatal. Nevertheless, Maximus has his revenge. He kills Commodus before dying in the arena himself.

An exciting story indeed, made all the more powerful by the convincing way the role of Maximus is played by

Russell Crowe and Commodus by Joaquin Phoenix. But the question that arose in my mind after watching this blockbuster was whether the audience would be any the wiser as far as the history of the period is concerned. If Ridley Scott's intention was to show that Roman society was remarkably violent, then he certainly succeeded. If he wanted to show that Commodus was a cruel emperor, devoid of any sense of justice, then he achieved this too. But if with his portrayal of Maximus and the fights in the Colosseum he wanted to show how gladiator fights were staged, then I can only conclude that his film is nothing less than a distortion of the truth.

The filmmakers made things harder for themselves by inventing their own protagonist to rise up against the despised Commodus rather than taking an existing story as their starting point. General Maximus never existed, he is a creation of the scriptwriters, who for the sake of the narrative resorted to contingencies that directly contradict the traditional stories found in the sources. Take the character of Commodus. However bad he may have been, he was not his own father's murderer. Emperor Marcus Aurelius died a natural death either as the result of extreme exhaustion or from an infectious disease that had already claimed many victims. As far back as AD 177 he named Commodus as one of his regents, so the son was expected to succeed the father in the usual way. It is equally impossible to imagine that Marcus Aurelius ever talked about restoring the republic. In the late second century the imperial system, following the benign rule of the emperors Trajan, Hadrian, Antoninus Pius and Marcus Aurelius, was not under discussion. There was no question of returning to the republican system. Everyone, even the senators who were looking forward to Commodus' death, knew that it would be utopian to think about re-establishing a republican government. The way Commodus dies in the film represents an even greater departure from the facts as we know them. In the film he is killed in the arena by Maximus, two or three years after the death of Marcus Aurelius. In reality Commodus only became the victim of a palace revolt more than ten years later, in AD 192.

Many of the reviews of *Gladiator* point out that the filmmakers did all they could to present the realities of the ancient world as accurately as possible. This may be the case, but if we look at a few of the Latin names and designations it becomes clear that they did not take advice from anyone with even a modest knowledge of the Latin language. The gladiator manager (*lanista*), magnificently played by Oliver Reed, is called Proximo in the film, although in correct Latin his name would have to have been Proximus. The inscription over the entrance to the gladiator school in Rome is even more garbled. It reads LUDUS MAGNUS GLADIATORES (great school gladiators), whereas it should read LUDUS MAGNUS GLADIATORUM (great school of the gladiators) or LUDUS MAGNUS GLADIATORIUS (great gladiatorial school).

From the way Commodus is depicted in the film it is obvious that little attention was paid to the impression people had of him in ancient times. In the film he is a pale, rather effeminate weakling with dark hair and bags under his eyes. In reality he must have been a vigorous-looking man with bleached locks. He was in the habit of dressing up as Hercules, with a lion's skin and a heavy cudgel, and he fought in the arena on many occasions as a *secutor*, with a sword in his left hand. There is some room for dispute about how successful he was as a gladiator, but there is no doubt he had extensive experience as a combatant in the arena. His fight with Maximus should have been staged quite differently, with Commodus as a *secutor*. Consequently, Maximus would have had to fight as a *retiarius*. But the filmmakers decided against this. Maximus appears in the arena with a small round shield and armour that was worn by Roman soldiers but not by gladiators.

The film has a cavalier attitude when it comes to the gladiators' weapons. We have seen that gladiators almost always specialised in one kind of weapon and that all the various types of gladiator had their own specific equipment. There is little indication of this in *Gladiator*. The weapons bear little resemblance to the daggers, swords, helmets and leg-plates found at Pompeii, or to the weapons depicted in ancient artworks. It seems clear that the filmmakers, keen to make the fully armed gladiators look as spectacular as possible, chose weapons from a wide range of historical periods. Marcus Junkelmann, the highly respected expert on gladiator weapons, has identified in the film Corinthian helmets from the earliest times, hoplite shields from the fifth and fourth centuries BC, Roman military armour, Viking and Turkish helmets, and breastplates that look very much like late-mediaeval chain mail.[175]

The parts of the film that give the viewer the most misleading impression of all are the fight scenes. At one point we see Maximus fighting another gladiator who is wearing a fantasy mask and multicoloured armour made up of small plates like scales. At the same time he has half an eye on a tiger that has suddenly appeared in the arena. In the background is a small pillar that did not exist in the Colosseum but was erected in the Circus

Maximus at the point where the chariots would turn during races. This fight is nothing less than a combination of a broad selection of events on the programme of a day at the Colosseum, which would have occurred in sequence but never at the same time. By having Maximus fight a tiger as well as a gladiator, gladiatorial combat is divested of its rules, in fact it is reduced to a chaotic free for all. And if there is one thing that has, I hope, become clear in the course of this book, it is that although the organisers were constantly trying to provide even more spectacle and variety, they did so within certain firm constraints. Single combat between two men was always the high point of a day at the Colosseum. The fact that the filmmakers opted for a fantasy spectacle shows that they had no intention of being faithful to historical 'reality'. This is regrettable, because it means they passed up the opportunity to present gladiator fights in an authentic context, using all the sophisticated technical aids now available.

Epilogue

I began this book by asking myself how I would have behaved if I had witnessed a gladiator show in the Colosseum. Now, after spending nearly two years in the world of the gladiators, the same question remains. I have not found the answer. In fact, I feel more ambivalent than ever, and find myself vacillating between the attitudes of the world in which I live and the world of the Romans. Daydreaming at my desk, feeling secure in a society where we are free to express our condemnation of violent spectacle openly and unambiguously, it is easy to convince myself that a single performance would have been more than enough for me.

On the other hand, suppose I had grown up in Rome, an environment in which violence played a decisive role, where might was right, not only in the army but in civilian life too. Would I have felt the same way? Would I have behaved differently from the vast majority of Romans? Would I have loathed the bloodthirsty shows and sympathised with Tacitus, who made no secret of his disapproval of what went on in the arena? Or would I have felt more like Cicero or Seneca, in whose comments I detect a certain ambivalence, a deep disdain for the mass hysteria of the terraces mixed with admiration for the courage of a brave gladiator? Or would I, along with the emperor, the senators, the Vestal Virgins and all those many other spectators, have cheered the very cruelties that now make me feel nothing but shame.

Of course it is an impossible question. I could easily evade it by saying that I will never, under any circumstances, be able to comprehend the gruesome acts that were perpetrated in the arena. A number of historians, and I named several of them in my introduction, have made statements of this kind. But I must honestly say that I have little sympathy for scholars who, like moral crusaders, measure the gladiator fights against modern standards of behaviour as a way of discharging their own sense of moral outrage. It is a form of 'ethically correct behaviour' inspired by the spirit of our own age, and it does not do justice to the phenomenon of the gladiator shows and the role played in Roman society by this form of popular entertainment.

It is misleading to study the gladiator fights as if they were an isolated phenomenon, an excrescence, a dark page in the otherwise illustrious history of Rome. Roman society was soaked in violence. Its presence could be felt everywhere. Rome had achieved greatness by winning wars through excessive violence. The historian William Harris writes of the pathological regularity with which Rome went to war and the extreme cruelty that was involved, greater than that of any other people in the ancient Mediterranean world.[176] Roman vocabulary simply did not include the word compassion. Protest and opposition were always put down with a heavy hand. The men who committed these extreme acts of violence were ordinary Roman soldiers, farm boys from the countryside. Under the leadership of officers who would later play a prominent role in politics, they worked towards making Rome great and extending its fame and its territory. They regarded no means of achieving these goals as excessive, even if it cost them their own lives. Thousands of Roman soldiers died for this ideal. Anyone who refused to co-operate suffered the same fate as their defeated enemies. Any soldier the leadership regarded as having behaved in a cowardly manner was executed by his fellow soldiers on orders from above. Defeated enemies were killed or sold as slaves. The strongest among them were selected to fight in the arena the way the Romans believed battles should be fought: bravely, with no respect for death and with absolute determination to achieve a famous victory. So the arena became an extension of the battlefield.

At the end of the republican period, by which time Rome had a firm grip on the Mediterranean world and fewer military campaigns were necessary, the amphitheatre became the place where the Romans could express themselves with abandon, where they could indulge their passion for bloodletting and ruthless combat. In the arenas of Rome and provincial towns, the war was played out again repeatedly, in all its cruelty and violence, while the emperor and the people looked on. These macabre shows brought them together, shows in which they were the winners and the gladiators were the losers, although some men might perhaps be able to fight their way back into a society that had rejected them. The Romans, brought up on warfare, fame, power and violence, saw nothing wrong with the gladiator shows. They were reminders of the past, and they illustrated time and again the fact that the emperor was the ruler of an immense empire and everyone was duty-bound to obey him. It was no accident that the gladiator shows and the emperor cult developed in parallel in the provinces. Amphitheatres that towered above the towns provided a suitable setting for the cult. Would the Romans have built such colossal facilities all over the empire if the games were only an incidental phenomenon? And could the games have grown so popular if they had not been so firmly rooted in Roman society? Tacitus, who hated gladiators, was probably right when he wrote about Rome, 'There are a number of vices typical of this city that children learn more or less at their mother's knee: a fondness for the theatre and a passion for chariot races and gladiator shows.'[177]

The shows had a seemingly irresistible appeal. In his Colosseum letter, Seneca points to the fact that an unwary spectator could easily be sucked into the maelstrom of enthusiasm. In my introduction I describe a case in which this actually happened. Augustine's pupil Alypius resolved to watch a gladiator show with a critical eye, but afterwards he was forced to admit he had failed. He had allowed himself to get carried away by the enthusiasm of the galleries, he had cheered and jeered along with the other spectators and left the amphitheatre a fanatical supporter of gladiatorial combat (see pages 10–11). When he visited the arena as a spectator, Alypius already knew what he could expect to see there from stories told by eyewitnesses. He was convinced he would be able to resist. Yet in spite of the wise lessons taught him by Augustine, he could not remain true to himself in the turbid atmosphere of the amphitheatre. Who am I to say that, no matter what the circumstances, I would have been capable of resisting the appeal of the Colosseum?

Glossary

andabata gladiator who fought blindfold

auctoratus gladiator who had voluntarily signed a contract (*auctoramentum*) with a gladiator manager

bestiarius man who fought wild animals

bustiarius gladiator who performed at funerals

carnarium literally, meat room, mortuary

cavea tiers of seating in the amphitheatre

cena libera free meal the evening before a gladiator show

contraretiarius gladiator deployed to fight a *retiarius*, often a *secutor*

crematio sentence of death by fire

damnatio ad bestias sentence of death by wild animals

damnatio ad flammas sentence of death by fire

damnatio ad gladium sentence of death by the sword

dimachaerus (probably) gladiator with two swords

doctor trainer

edicta muneris wall posters used to advertise gladiator shows

editor man who organised and conducted games on behalf of the emperor

eques fighter who started off on horseback and then continued on foot

essedarius gladiator who fought from a chariot

familia gladiatoria group of gladiators in a school under the control of a gladiator manager *ferra acuta* sharp offensive weapons

gallus early type of gladiator

gladius sword

gregarius cheapest category of gladiator

gregatim fights involving many gladiators at once

hasta lance

'hoc habet' 'he has it', shouted by the public when a gladiator had received a fatal thrust

hoplomachus a heavily armoured gladiator who fought mainly with a lance

hordearii barley-porridge eaters, insulting term for gladiators

hypogeum passageways, pens and cells under the arena

iaculum a throwing spear

iugulare to cut someone's throat, to kill

lanista gladiator manager, agent who dealt in gladiators

laquaerius gladiator who used a lasso

ludus 1. festival with theatrical events and chariot races in honour of a particular deity
2. gladiator school

missio, *missus* defeated gladiator who was allowed to leave the arena alive

munerarius person who put up the money for a gladiator show

munus, pl. *munera* gladiator show, originally an obligation towards an important person who had died

murmillo a type of gladiator with a large, long shield, often put up against a *retiarius*

naumachia re-enacted sea battle on an artificial lake or in an amphitheatre

noxius a person sentenced to die in a shameful manner

paegnarius gladiator who fought with wooden weapons

palus pole used in exercises with wooden weapons. The titles *primus palus, secundus palus* and so on indicated the quality of the gladiator

parma small shield

podium balcony, box for honoured guests in the amphitheatre

pollice verso the turning of thumbs (up or down) by the crowd to indicate a gladiator should be killed

pompa opening procession

porta Libitinaria gate through which bodies were carried out of the arena

porta Sanavivaria gate through which the winners and survivors left the arena

probatio armorum inspection of the weapons

prolusio warm-up act in which the gladiators used wooden weapons

provocator type of gladiator with heavy weapons

pugio dagger

retiarius gladiator with net and trident

rudis wooden sword

sagittarius gladiator who fought with bow and arrow

samnis probably the most ancient type of gladiator

scutum large shield

secutor literally, pursuer, a type of gladiator put up against a *retiarius*

sica curved sword

spoliarium room where equipment was removed from dead gladiators

stans missus both gladiators leave the arena after an undecided fight

summa rudis wooden sword given to a gladiator when he was allowed to leave the gladiator school a free man *thraex* heavily armoured gladiator with a curved sword, deployed even as far back as the republic

tiro recruit

tridens trident

vela awnings

venatio the chasing of wild animals

venator man who fought animals, huntsman

veteranus veteran, experience fighter

List of Amphitheatres

Scattered across the Roman Empire were more than 200 amphitheatres, large and small, almost half of them in what is now Italy. The most important are listed here. The list is based on Hönle and Henze (1981) and on Golvin and Landes (1990) and I have tried to include as many as possible of the amphitheatres whose remains can still be seen. Where possible, I have indicated the external dimensions of the amphitheatre and the size of the arena, to the nearest metre. I have not included combined theatres that were used for more than one purpose.

Albenga (Northern Italy), third century. Arena: 70 by 50 metres

Albano Laziale (Central Italy), *c.* AD 200. Arena: 67 by 45 metres

Ancona (Northeastern Italy), *c.* AD 120. Exterior: 111 by 97 metres

Arezzo (Central Italy), *c.* AD 100. Exterior: 121 by 92 metres

Arles (Southern France), *c.* AD 80. Exterior: 136 by 107 metres. Arena: 72 by 43 metres

Augst (Switzerland), *c.* AD 150. Arena: 48 by 33 metres

Avenches (Switzerland), late first century AD. Exterior: 115 by 87 metres. Arena: 59 by 37 metres

Bordeaux (France), third century AD. Exterior: 132 by 110 metres. Arena: 69 by 46 metres

Budapest (Hungary), mid-second century AD. Exterior: 130 by 107 metres

Cagliari (Sardinia), second century AD. Arena: 47 by 31 metres

Capua (Italy), AD 70–80. Exterior: 170 by 140 metres

Catania (Sicily), c. AD 240. Arena: 51 metres long

Carthage (Tunisia), first and second century AD. Exterior: 156 by 128 metres. Arena: 66 by 36 metres

Cimiez (France), first quarter of third century AD. Exterior: 65 by 54 metres. Arena: 45 by 34 metres

El Djem (Tunisia), c. AD 230. Exterior: 149 by 124 metres. Arena: 65 metres long

Frascati (Central Italy), mid-second century AD. Exterior: 80 by 53 metres. Arena: 47 by 29 metres

Fréjus (Southern France), c. AD 100. Exterior: 114 by 82 metres. Arena: 68 by 39 metres

Grotte di Nocera Superiore (Southern Italy), second half of first century AD. Exterior: 125 by 102 metres

Italica (Spain), c. AD 90. Exterior: 156 metres long. Arena: 71 by 46 metres

Lebda/Leptis Magna (Libya), c. AD 60. Exterior: approximately 100 by 80 metres

Lecce (Southern Italy), first century AD. Exterior: 102 by 83 metres. Arena: 51 by 38 AD

Limoges (France), early second century AD. Exterior: 138 by 116 metres

Lucera (Southern Italy), c. AD 100. Exterior: 133 by 99 metres. Arena: 75 by 46 metres

Lyon (France), 19 BC to c. AD 20 and c. AD 80. Exterior: 140 by 117 metres. Arena: 64 by 41 metres

Mérida (Spain), 8 BC. Exterior: 126 by 102 metres. Arena: 64 by 41 metres

Milan (Italy), c. AD 80. Exterior: 155 by 125 metres

Nîmes (France), *c.* AD 80. Exterior: 132 by 101 metres. Arena: 69 by 38 metres

Paestum (Italy), first half of first century AD. Exterior: 100 by 65 metres

Périgueux (France), early first century AD. Arena: 65 by 40 metres

Petronel/Carnuntum (Austria), *c.* AD 130. Arena: 68 by 50 metres

Pompeii (Italy), *c.* 80 BC. Exterior: 135 by 104 metres

Pozzuoli/Puteoli (Italy), last quarter of first century BC. Exterior: 130 by 95 metres

Pozzuoli/Puteoli (Italy), *c.* AD 80. Exterior: 149 by 116 metres. Arena: 75 by 42 metres

Pula (Slovenia), AD 80–100. Exterior: 132 by 105 metres. Arena: 68 by 42 metres

Rimini (Italy), late first century AD. Exterior: 118 by 88 metres. Arena: 74 by 44 metres

Rome (Italy), AD 70–80. Exterior: 188 by AD 156. Arena: 80 by 54 metres

Saintes (France), *c.* AD 60. Exterior: 125 by 102 metres. Arena: 64 by 39 metres

Split (Croatia), *c.* AD 200. Exterior: 110 by 125 metres. Arena: 64 by 40 metres

Sutri (Italy), 53 BC. Exterior: 55 by 45 metres

Syracuse (Sicily), early third century AD. Exterior: 141 by 118 metres. Arena: 69 by 39 metres

Tarragona (Spain), AD 80. Arena: 62 by 67 metres

Trier (Germany), *c.* AD 100. Exterior: 140 by 120 metres

Verona (Italy), AD 70–80. Exterior: 152 by 103 metres. Arena: 74 by 44 metres

Windisch (Switzerland), *c.* AD 300. Exterior: 112 by 98 metres

Xanten (Germany), *c.* AD 100. Exterior: 100 by 87 metres

References

1   Juvenal, *Satires* 10, 78-81
2   Grant 1971, p. 8
3   Carcopino 1987, p. 300
4   Ville 1981, p. 471
5   Balsdon 1969, p. 308
6   Barton 1993, p. 11
7   Paoli 1958, p. 253
8   Friedländer 1920, p. 94
9   GA Amsterdam, *Keurboek Q*: F 179, as quoted in Spierenburg 1990, p. 232
10 Augustine, *Confessions* 6, 8, 13
11 His account of the origins of the gladiator fights comes to us through the work of the third-century author Athenaeus, *Deipnosophistae* 4, 153f-154a
12 Isidorus, *Origines* 10, 247
13 Tertullian, *Ad nationes* 1, 10, 47 and *Apologeticum* 15, 5; see also Wiedemann 1992, p. 30
14 Tertullian, *De Spectaculis* 12, 1-4
15 Festus, 134b: 22; here I follow Barton 1993, p.13-15; 23-24; 40-46
16 See among others Ville 1981, p. 9-19 and Potter in Potter and Mattingly 1999, p. 305-306
17 Livy, *The History of Rome from its Foundation* 1, 35, 9
18 Tacitus, *Annals* 1, 77
19 Pliny the Elder, *Natural History* 8, 6, 17

20   Livy, *The History of Rome from its Foundation* 39, 22, 2

21   *Ibid.* 44, 18, 8

22   Valerius Maximus 2, 4, 7; Livy, *Epitome* 16

23   Livy, *The History of Rome from its Foundation* 23, 30

24   *Ibid.* 31, 50

25   *Ibid.* 39, 46

26   *Ibid.* 41, 28

27   Plutarch, *Gaius Gracchus* 12

28   Suetonius, *Emperors of Rome, Julius Caesar* 39

29   Cassius Dio, *History of Rome* 47, 40

30   Plutarch, *Crassus* 8 and following; Florus, *Short History of Rome* 2, 8

31   Augustus, *The Deeds of the Divine Augustus* 22

32   Suetonius, *Emperors of Rome, Augustus* 43

33   Tacitus, *Annals* 4, 62

34   Suetonius, *Emperors of Rome, Claudius* 21, 5

35   Suetonius, *Emperors of Rome, Nero* 11

36   *Ludus* can mean either 'game' or 'festival', as in *ludi circenses* (circus games). But it can also mean 'school'. A *ludus gladiatorius* is a gladiator school.

37   Cicero, *The Tusculum Disputations* 2, 17, 41

38   Seneca, *De Tranquilitate* 11, 1–6

39   Tertullian, *De Spectaculis* 21

40   Lucianus, *Toxaris* 58

41   Robert 1940, p. 286

42   Suetonius, *Emperors of Rome, Julius Caesar* 39

43   Cassius Dio, *History of Rome* 51, 22, 4

44   *Ibid.* 56, 25, 7

45   *Ibid.* 57, 14, 3

46   Juvenal, *Satires* 8, 200–210

47   Cassius Dio, *History of Rome* 73, 19, 5

48 *Ibid.* 73, 21, 2

49 Herodianus, *Historia de imperio post Marcum* 1, 15, 108

50 For a detailed account of Commodus as a gladiator, see Hekster 2002, pp. 137–162

51 Cassius Dio, *History of Rome* 76, 8, 2–3

52 Galen, *Peri trophon Dynameos* 1, 19

53 Vegetius, *The Military Institutions of the Romans* 1, 11–12

54 *Inscriptiones Latinae Selectae* 7559

55 *Corpus Inscriptionum Latinarum* 6, 631–632

56 Seneca, *Letter* 70, 20

57 Symmachus, *Letter* 2, 46

58 Ville 1981, pp. 318–325; see also Junkelmann 2000, pp. 142–3

59 *Inscriptiones Latinae Selectae* 5107

60 *Ibid.* 5083, see also Wiedemann 1992, pp. 121–122

61 *Ibid.* 5088

62 *Ibid.* 5113

63 *Ibid.* 5106

64 For these and other statistics see Ville 1981, pp. 321–2

65 *Inscriptiones Latinae Selectae* 5115

66 Robert 1940, p. 131 no. 79

67 *Corpus Inscriptionum Latinarum* 4, 4353; 4, 8916; 4, 4342

68 Barton 1996, p. 73

69 Juvenal, *Satires* 6, 103–13

70 *Historia Augusta, Marcus Aurelius* 19, 7

71 Cassius Dio, *History of Rome* 60, 28, 2

72 *Corpus Inscriptionum Latinarum* 9, 2237

73 Juvenal, *Satires* 6, 247–264

74 The text of the inscription from Italica is *Corpus*

Inscriptionum Latinarum 2, 6278; I have taken this table from Potter and Mattingly 1999, pp. 318-19.The standard work is J.H. Oliver and R.E.A. Palmer, 'Minutes of an act of the Roman Senate', *Hesperia* 24 (1955) p. 320-49

75 *Inscriptiones Latinae Selectae* 1738
76 Suetonius, *Emperors of Rome, Tiberius* 7
77 Suetonius, *Emperors of Rome, Nero* 30
78 Horace, *Letter* 1, 1, 4
79 *Inscriptiones Latinae Selectae* 5163, 45-46
80 Martial, *Epigrams* 5, 24, 9
81 Seneca, *De beneficiis* 6, 12, 2
82 Martial, *Epigrams* 24, 11-14
83 Isidorus of Seville, *Origines* 18, 53-55
84 Pliny the Elder, *Natural History* 36, 116-120
85 Cassius Dio, *History of Rome* 43, 22, 4
86 Five of the seven wonders of the world are named here. Those not mentioned are the palace of Ecbatana and the Temple of Olympia (or the Colossus of Rhodes).
87 Martial, *Liber de Spectaculis* 1
88 *Ibid.* 2
89 Opinions differ as regards this system of lifts. I draw on Cozzo 1971, pp. 59-72; see also Rea in Gabucci 2001, p. 224
90 Martialis, *Liber de Spectaculis* 3
91 Tacitus, *Annals* 14, 17
92 It is possible that the building of this amphitheatre started earlier, under Nero.
93 Pliny the Elder, *Natural History* 8, 20, 53
94 *Ibid.* 8, 7, 19
95 *Ibid.* 8, 24, 64 and 8, 40, 96
96 *Ibid.* 8, 20, 53 and 8, 24, 64; Cassius Dio, *History of*

Rome 39, 38, 2

97   *Ibid*. 8, 20, 53 and 8, 70, 182

98   *Ibid*. 8, 24, 64; Cassius Dio, *History of Rome* 55, 10, 7–8 and 56, 27, 4–5

99   Cassius Dio, *History of Rome* 60, 7, 3 and 61, 91, 1

100 *Ibid*. 66, 25, 1

101 *Ibid*. 68, 15

102 *Historia Augusta, Antoninus Pius* 10, 9

103 *Historia Augusta, Gordiani Tres* 3

104 *Ibid*. 33

105 *Historia Augusta, Probus* 19

106 *Anthologia Palatina* 7, 626

107 *L'Année épigraphique* 1967, pg. 549; see also Gabucci 2001, pg. 66

108 *Price Edict of Diocletian* 34; Lauffer, Berlin 1971

109 For mention of the *usarii*, inscriptions and other literary references, see Gabucci 2001, p. 65 and Bomgardner 2000, p. 212

110 Pliny the Elder, *Natural History* 8, 3, 6

111 Juvenal, *Satires* 10, 78–81

112 *Corpus Inscriptionum Latinarum* 4, 3884

113 Statius, Silvae 2, 5

114 Cassius Dio, *History of Rome* 77, 1, 4

115 Lucina was a Roman goddess of birth.

116 Martial, *Liber de Spectaculis* 12–14

117 Seneca, *De brevitate vitae* 13, 6; Pliny the Elder, *Natural History* 8, 7, 20–21; Cassius Dio, *History of Rome* 39, 38, 2–4

118 Martial, *Liber de Spectaculis* 23

119 *Ibid*. 15

120 Seneca, *Letter* 70, 23

121 After AD 212, when the distinction between the various categories of free people was abandoned

with the introduction of the *Constitutio Antoniniana* (they all became Roman citizens), a new definition of status was introduced. Death by the sword was reserved for condemned *honestiores* (senators, imperial functionaries and town councillors), while the rest (*humiliores*) were sentenced to death by wild animals or by fire.

122 Ignatius, *Letter to the Romans* 5

123 Martial, *Liber de Spectaculis* 21

124 *Ibid.* 5

125 *Ibid.* 8

126 *Ibid.* 7

127 Tertullian, *The Sufferings of the Holy Perpetua and Felicitas* 19, 5

128 Aulus Gellius, *The Attic Nights* 5, 14, 10 and 17, 27

129 Tertullian, *Apologeticum* 15, 4 tells us that this ritual was also performed for dead gladiators, but this seems unlikely. Dead gladiators made a more honourable exit.

130 Suetonius, *Emperors of Rome, Claudius* 21, 6

131 *Corpus Inscriptionum Latinarum* 4, 10238

132 *Ibid.* 4, 10236

133 Quintilia, *Declamationes* 9, 6

134 Martial, *Liber de Spectaculis* 27

135 Junkelmann 2000, pp. 138–139

136 Suetonius, *Emperors of Rome, Domitian* 9

137 Tertullian, *Apologeticum* 15, 4

138 Cassius Dio, *History of Rome* 66, 25, 4–5

139 *Ibid.* 66, 25

140 Suetonius, *Emperors of Rome, Julius Caesar* 39, 2

141 In the film *Gladiator*, the Battle of Zama in 202 BC is staged in front of an audience. In this famous battle at the end of the Second Punic War, the

Romans dealt a final blow to the Carthaginians on African soil. In the film the gladiator Maximus and his fellow fighters, who play the Carthaginians, defeat the men playing Romans, which elicits from Commodus the cutting remark that he had always thought it went the other way.

142 Suetonius, *Emperors of Rome, Julius Caesar* 39, 4

143 The bireme was rowed by two rows of oarsmen, one above the other, the trireme by three rows on three different levels. The quadrireme was rowed by two or three rows of oarsmen, one above the other. The difference between this and the bireme and the trireme was that instead of each having his own oar, the oarsmen on the quadrireme sat one or two an oar. A quadrireme was rowed on two levels, had two oarsmen per oar on the lower level and two per oar on the higher level. If the quadrireme had oarsmen on three levels, the arrangement was one-one-two.

144 Augustus, *The Deeds of the Divine Augustus* 23

145 Tacitus, *Annals* 12, 56

146 Suetonius, *Emperors of Rome, Claudius* 21

147 Tacitus, *Annals* 12, 56, 3

148 Cassius Dio, *History of Rome* 59, 10, 5

149 *Ibid.* 61, 9, 5

150 *Ibid.* 64, 25, 4

151 Martial is of course referring to Caesar Titus

152 Martial, *Liber de Spectaculis* 30

153 The thrust of this chapter is based partly on Kyle 1998. He was the first person to investigate systematically the ways in which corpses and carcasses may have been processed.

154 Suetonius, *Emperors of Rome, Caligula* 27

155 Apuleius, *Metamorphoses* 4, 13–14

156 Flavius Josephus, *Jewish Antiquities* 19, 130

157 Tertullian, *Apologeticum* 9, 11

158 Cicero, *The Tusculum Disputations* 2, 17, 41

159 Cicero, *Letters to his Friends* 7, 1

160 Cicero, *Pro Sestio* 106

161 Seneca, *Letter To Lucilius* 7

162 Tacitus, *Annals* 1, 76, 3 The passages by Tacitus on gladiators can be found in Wistrand 1992, pp. 26–8 and 93, note 59

163 Clement of Alexandria, *Paedagogus* 3, 11, 77

164 Tertullian, *Adversus Marcianum* 1, 27, 5

165 This theory is explored in detail by Wiedemann 1992, pp. 155–6 and Wiedemann 1995

166 *Codex Theodosianus* 15, 12. 1

167 *Chronica, Monumenta Germaniae Historica, auctores Antiquissimi* 9. 300

168 The Venerable Bede, *Collectanea* 1, 3

169 I have based this passage on Rea in Gabucci (ed.) 2001, p. 207

170 I have not studied Monaldeschi's account but have based this passage on Rea in Gabucci (ed.) 2001, p. 200

171 I have taken both these examples from Woodward 2001

172 François-René de Chateaubriand, *Correspondance générale* I (1789–1807)

173 I found this anecdote in Woodward 2001

174 Solomon 2001, p. 55

175 Junkelmann 2000, pp. 8–9

176 Harris 1979, 11, p. 51–53

177 Tacitus, *Dialogue on Rhetoricians*, 29

Bibliography

Here I list only the books and articles I have consulted regularly. Publications on more incidental subjects are included only if I have laid particular emphasis on their findings.

R. Auguet, *Cruelty and Civilization: The Roman Games*, London 1972 (translation of *Cruauté et civilisation: les jeux romains*, Paris 1970)

D.Aumenti, *Spettacoli del Colosseo nelle cronache degli Antichi*, Rome 2001

A. Baker, *The Gladiator. The Secret History of Rome's Warrior Slaves*, London 2000

J.P.V.D. Balsdon, *Life and Leisure in Ancient Rome*, London 1969

C.A. Barton, *The Sorrows of the Ancient Romans. The Gladiator and the Monster*, Princeton 1993

D.L. Bomgardner, *The Story of the Roman Amphitheatre*, London and New York 2000

K.R. Bradley, *Slavery and Rebellion in the Roman World, 140 BC–70 BC*, London 1989

A. Cameron, *Bread and Circuses. The Roman Emperor and his People*, Oxford 1974

J. Carcopino, *Het dagelijks leven in het oude Rome*, Utrecht 1987 (translation of *La vie quotidienne à Rome à l'apogée de l' Empire*, Paris 1939)

K.M. Coleman, 'Fatal charades: Roman executions staged

as mythological enactments', *Journal of Roman Studies* 80 (1990) 44–73

— 'Launching into history: Aquatic displays in the early empire', *Journal of Roman Studies* 83 (1993) 48–74

G. Cozzo, *The Colosseum. The Flavian Amphitheatre. Architecture, Building Techniques. History of the Construction. Plan of Works*, Rome 1971

L. Friedländer, *Darstellungen aus der Sittengeschichte Roms in der Zeit von August bis zum Ausgang der Antonine*, Vol. 2, Leipzig 1920

A. Futrell, *Blood in the Arena. The Spectacle of Roman Power*, Austin 1997

A. Gabucci (ed.), *The Colosseum*, Los Angeles 2001

J.-C. Golvin, *L'amphithéâtre romain*, Paris 1988

J.-C. Golvin and C. Landes, *Amphithéâtres et gladiateurs*, Rome 1990

M. Grant, *Gladiators*, London 1971

W.V. Harris, *War and Imperialism in Republican Rome 327–70 BC*, Oxford 1979

O. Hekster, *Commodus. An Emperor at the Crossroads*, Amsterdam 2002

A. Hönle and A. Henze, *Römische Amphitheater und Stadien*, Zürich 1981

K. Hopkins, 'Murderous Games', in his *Death and Renewal. Sociological Studies in Roman History*, Vol. 2, 1–30, Cambridge 1983

G. Jennison, *Animals for Show and Pleasure in Ancient Rome*, Manchester 1937

E. Köhne, C. Ewigleben and R. Jackson (eds.), *Gladiators and Caesars. The Power of Spectacle in Ancient Rome*, London 2000

M. Junkelmann, *Das Spiel mit dem Tod. So kämpften Roms Gladiatoren*, Mainz am Rhein 2000

D.G. Kyle, *Spectacles of Death in Ancient Rome*, London and New York 1998

J. Lendering, *Stad in marmer. Gids voor het antieke Rome aan de hand van tijdgenoten*, Amsterdam 2002

D. Mancioli, *Giochi e spettacoli. Vita e costumi dei Romani antichi* (part 4), Rome 1987

D.P. Mannix, *The Way of the Gladiator*, New York 2001 (new edition of *Those About to Die*, New York 1958)

U. Paoli, *Rome: Its People, Life and Customs*, New York 1958

P. Plass, *The Game of Death in Ancient Rome. Arena Sport and Political Suicide*, Wisconsin 1995

D.S. Potter and D.J. Mattingly (eds.), *Life, Death and Entertainment in the Roman Empire*, Ann Arbor 1999

A. La Regina (ed.), *Sangue e Arena*, Rome 2001

L. Robert, *Les gladiateurs dans l'Orient grec*, Paris 1940

F. Savi, *I gladiatori. Storia organizzazione iconografie*, Rome 1980

A. Scobie, 'Spectator security and comfort at gladiatorial games', *Nikephoros. Zeitschrift für Sport und Kultur im Altertum* 1 (1988) 191-244

J. Solomon, *The Ancient World in the Cinema*, New Haven and London 2001

P. Spierenburg, *De verbroken betovering. Mentaliteitsgeschiedenis van preïndustrieel Europa*, Hilversum 1990

J.C.M. Toynbee, *Animals in Roman Life and Art*, London 1973

G. Ville, 'Les jeux de gladiateurs dans l'empire chrétien', *Mélanges d'archéologie et d'histoire publiés par l'école française de Rome* 62 (1960) 273-335

— *La gladiature en occident des origines à la mort de*

Domitien, Rome 1981

T. Wiedemann, *Emperors and Gladiators*, London and New York 1992

— 'Das Ende der römischen Gladiatorenspiele', *Nikephoros. Zeitschrift für Sport und Kultur im Altertum 8* (1995) 145-159

M. Wistrand, *Entertainment and Violence in Ancient Rome. The Attitudes of Roman Writers in the First Century AD*, Göteborg 1992

C. Woodward, *In Ruins*, London 2001

Index

Marcellus, theatre of 20, 212, 218
Marcus Antonius, consul 40
Marcus Aurelius, Emperor 20, 47, 56, 73, 79, 82, 226, 227, 228, 229
Mars, god 19, 179
Martial, poet 88, 99, 100, 107, 137, 140, 144, 146, 147, 154, 155, 156, 181
Mauretania 65
Mausoleum of Augustus 99, 212
Maximus, fictional general in film, gladiator 9, 226, 227, 228, 229, 230, 231
Maximus, governor 202
Mediolanum Santonum *see* Saintes 98
Mediterranean Sea 130
Meleager, mythological figure 147
Memmius, Lucius, builder of theatre 20
Memphis 99
Mercury, god 14, 159, 172, 173
Mérida 99
Messalina, wife of Claudius 75, 107
Metellus, Caecilius, consul 24
Milo, Titus Annius, radical politician 32

Minerva, goddess 19, 29
Minos, King of Crete 155
Minotaur, mythological figure 155
Mirabilia urbis Romae, mediaeval travel guide 210
Misenus 114
Monaldeschi, Ludovico Bonconte, writer 212
Murmillo 82, 90, 93, 164, 168, *169,* 171, 225/Murmillones 89, 90, *92,* 111, 167
Mus, Publius Decius, consul 51
Mussolini 217, 218

Naples 71, 114, 116
Nasamonians 125
Nasica, gladiator 25, 66
Naumachia 176
Nemausus *see* Nîmes 117
Neptune, god 19
Nereus, god 181
Nero, Emperor 37, 47, 76, 82, 99, 122, 180, 182, 220, 221, 225
Nicholas V, Pope 213
Nicolas of Damascus, writer 13
Nîmes 53, 117, 118
Nobilior, Fulvius, organiser of hunting show 24
Normans 212

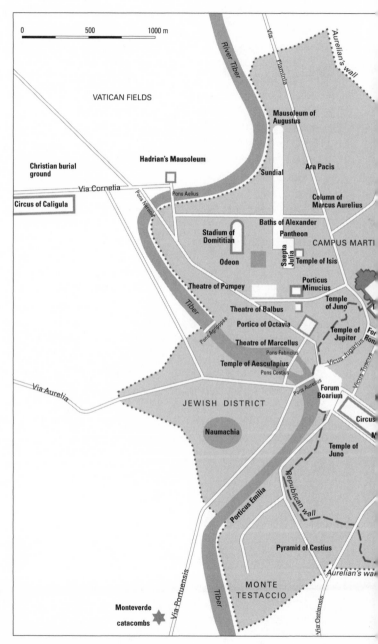

0   500   1000 m

River Tiber

Via Flaminia

Aurelian's wall

VATICAN FIELDS

Mausoleum of Augustus

Hadrian's Mausoleum

Christian burial ground

Sundial

Ara Pacis

Via Cornelia

Pons Aelius

Column of Marcus Aurelius

Pons Neronis

Circus of Caligula

Baths of Alexander

Stadium of Domititian

Pantheon

CAMPUS MARTI

Odeon

Saepta Julia

Temple of Isis

Tiber

Theatre of Pompey

Porticus Minucius

Theatre of Balbus

Temple of Juno

Pons Agrippae

Portico of Octavia

Temple of Jupiter

For Rom

Theatre of Marcellus

Pons Fabricius

Vicus Jugarius

Via Aurelia

Temple of Aesculapius

Pons Cestius

Pons Aurelius

Forum Boarium

Vicus Tuscus

JEWISH DISTRICT

Circus M

Naumachia

Temple of Juno

Republican wall

Porticus Emilia

Pyramid of Cestius

Via Portuensis

Tiber

MONTE TESTACCIO

Aurelian's wa

Via Ostiensis

Monteverde catacombs

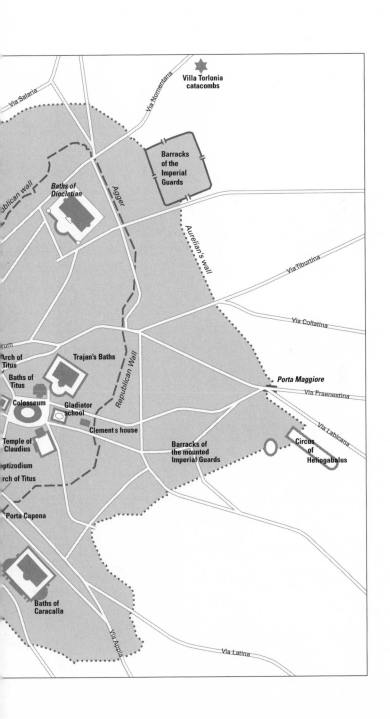

Via Salaria

Via Nomentana

★ Villa Torlonia catacombs

...ublican wall

Baths of Diocletian

Agger

Barracks of the Imperial Guards

Aurelian's wall

Via Tiburtina

Via Collatina

...rum

Arch of Titus

Trajan's Baths

Baths of Titus

Republican Wall

Porta Maggiore

Via Praenestina

Colosseum

Gladiator school

Clement's house

Temple of Claudius

...ptizodium

...rch of Titus

Barracks of the mounted Imperial Guards

Via Labicana

Circus of Heliogabalus

Porta Capena

Baths of Caracalla

Via Appia

Via Latina